D0732844

GREEK SALAD
A Dionysian Travelogue

Miles Lambert-Gócs

Ambeli Press
Williamsburg, Virginia

The Wine Appreciation Guild
San Francisco

Greek Salad: A Dionysian Travelogue

Published in the U.S. by:

Ambeli Press
1008 Settlement Drive
Williamsburg VA 23188
and
The Wine Appreciation Guild
360 Swift Avenue
South San Francisco CA 94080
(650) 866 3020
www.wineappreciation.com

Text copyright © 2004, Miles Lambert-Gócs

Library of Congress Control Number: 2004108180

Text by Miles Lambert-Gócs

ISBN: 1-891267-82-5

Printed in the United States of America

αφιερωμένο στην αγαπημένη μου κόρη,
Valerie

TABLE OF CONTENTS

PART I – AEGEAN ISLANDS

PART II – MAINLAND GREECE

PART III – IONIAN ISLANDS

PART I

AEGEAN ISLANDS

AEGEAN ISLANDS

(1) Tinos
(2) Andros
(3) Syros
(4) Paros
(5) Naxos
(6) Kythnos
(7) Serifos
(8) Sifnos/Milos
(9) Santorini
(10) Crete
(11) Samos
(12) Chios

1

SPIRITUAL REALM

I'm one of those poor souls who need the most vivid reminders of ancient Greece to be able to conjure it. Plying the Aegean Sea that for three millennia has remained the chief link between the Greek places scattered around it never fails me in that way. The airplane just will not do. I suppose sailboats must be the truest and swiftest means of transport back to Homer's world, but I settle for the ferries out of Piraeus.

I like to arrive in Piraeus while rosy-fingered dawn is still spreading over the Saronic Gulf. My habit is to catch an early cab from central Athens for a breezy ride down to the port. I am put in a seafaring mood on the way by radio reports giving the day's numerical Beaufort Scale readings on conditions throughout the Greek seas. These sunrise Beaufort reports are as much a background fixture of daily Aegean routine as 6 a.m. reports on Chicago Board of Trade corn and pork belly prices are in my own country, and give me pause to consider once again that becoming acquainted with Greece requires something of an amphibious spirit.

Across from the wharves along Akti Miaouli in Piraeus I pick up a flaky *bougatsa* pastry filled with sweetened semolina and flecked with powdered sugar, from a seller of ones that suit me just right. I pore over the steamship company menus of destinations while munching happily and letting the Aegean names enchant me. With physical character and the intangible element of mood differing markedly from one island to another, each possibility seems to offer a promise of who knows what. But no matter my landfall I can be sure the barnacles clinging to my encrusted faculties will be scraped away and the spontaneity that impelled Zorba to leap up from the deck upon spotting dolphins will be breathed back into me.

One mid-July day long after I was a seasoned Aegean hand I caught the ferry *Panayia Tinou* (Virgin of Tinos) for its namesake isle. The *meltemi*, the wind of summer drawn down from Russia by atmospheric play over North Africa, had begun blowing early in the season and the Beaufort reading for the northern Cyclades that day was up to 7, a moderate gale. Flocks of 'little sheep' (as the Greeks call whitecaps) ran endlessly over the Aegean, and the prow of the *Panayia Tinou* had been thoroughly washed with sea spray by the time we reached Tinos.

Whenever the *meltemi* shows up it lays a low cloud over the length of Tinos, with something of the effect of a nimbus, which apparently bestows a special aura on the island in the cosmology of the Aegean seafarer. Indeed the Greeks have always been susceptible to ascribing divine favor to Tinos. Both Aeolus the King of Winds and Poseidon the Sea-god were associated with Tinos in Homeric times. Later on, the 1st century A.D. geographer Strabo mentioned a temple of Poseidon that stood in a sacred precinct outside the city of Tinos and was the scene of an annual festival attended by a multitude of insular Greeks. The contemporary town of Chora similarly has been awash in pilgrims each August since 1823, when an icon of the Virgin Mary was discovered on Tinos by revelation. Worshipers seeking cures ascend, oftentimes on hands and knees, the arrow-straight street leading up the long, low hill from the port to the modern temple, the Church of *Panayia Evangelistrias*, where the miraculous icon is kept. The island's spell was cast over me too as the *Panayia Tinou* approached and I was captivated by the alignment of the harbor, the hill of Chora and the granite mountain of Exobourgo beyond, all under the nebular diadem placed by Aeolus.

A Greek couple from home, Babis and Anna Machairides, were on Tinos at the time visiting friends of theirs, the Christofilopouloses, whom I had met once at Babis and Anna's house in Washington. Neither Dr. Christofilopoulos nor his wife was from Tinos, but they had bought a summer home there in the certainty that they would be safe from the seamier side of Aegean tourism. Their faith was owing to the icon, which inspires the Tinians to take seriously their island's role as 'the Orthodox Lourdes.' Spirituality and wholesomeness reign on Tinos.

Dr. Christofilopoulos had no trouble arranging a room for me at the last minute. Tinos was still two

Greek Salad

weeks away from its annual period of hyper-prosperity around the Feast of the Virgin on August 15, when the logjam of pilgrims puts even street space for a sleeping mat at a premium. And foreigners, apparently put off by the Virgin and the faithful, rarely vie for Tinian mattresses, but prefer instead to maintain their libertarian vigil on neighboring Mykonos. I stayed where the Christofilopouloses have their mail delivered while on Tinos, the Aeolos Bay Hotel, across from a beach just outside Chora and on the road towards their house.

The remarkable asset of the Aeolos Bay was its owner, Andoni. I had an inkling that he was more than just another narrowly focused collector of drachmas when he drove me out to the Christofilopouloses' on my first evening. Andoni spoke American English as a result of having spent a year in San Diego while serving in the Greek Navy some years before he joined the ranks of insular innkeepers, and he expressed himself both with American idioms and word for word translations of Greek ones. He was especially colorful in digressing on the subject of religion after I mentioned having gone to see the Greek Orthodox icon that afternoon and noticed a Roman Catholic church on the way back to the Aeolos Bay. Andoni pointed out his quaintly Venetian surname, Prelorenzos, and noted spitefully that Tinos remains, to the consternation of the Orthodox hierarchy of Greece, the substantial Aegean stronghold of Catholicism that it has been ever since the Venetians controlled it during the Middle Ages. "And from Exobourgo to the rest of the island, where my village is, we are 'one hundred of one-hundred percent' Catholic."

I was ready to go to Exobourgo and beyond no matter the sectarian affiliations. The streets of Chora, chockablock with redundant sellers of votive candles, plastic vials for collecting holy water and rafts of Greek souvenir kitsch, worked no special charms on me, while the coveys of Greek matrons taking up café furniture in all directions on their way to or from the icon were more than I had bargained for in choosing Tinian piety over Mykonian iniquity. I was consider-ing an escape to the villages of Falatados and Steni after a shopkeeper said I could find wine on tap in those places. But Andoni objected when I aired that thought to him. He said that any wine I might find in the *taverna*s of Falatados and Steni likely would not even be from Tinos, such had been the decline in Tin-ian wine production in recent decades. If I was so in-terested in native wine, Andoni continued, I should come along with him the following day. My kind of traveler in the Aegean quickly learns to accept native proposals of that sort at face value.

Six of us set out about noon the next day, a Sun-day. I rode with Babis and Dr. Christofilopoulos in the doctor's safari vehicle, while Andoni with his wife and his sister led in a pickup truck. Andoni's dog, Rambo, the mascot of the Aeolos Bay and, despite his name, the docile recipient of the manhandling dished out by the guests' tots, had the run of the back of the pickup.

Greek Salad

Andoni fired up our curiosity by announcing with trumpets in his voice that he was going to show us "pre-history." I was sure I had no idea what he meant.

We drove into the mountains behind Chora, passed the turnoff for Falatados and Steni, and ascended further to the once imposing fortress of Exobourgo, which the Venetians did not surrender to the Turks until the early 18th century. Andoni pulled off to the side of the road near the ruins and signaled us to do likewise. He got out of the pickup and came to the driver's window to tell Dr. Christofilopoulos to follow the signposts for Volax. Volax? I wondered. My Greek islands guidebook that I had studied on the *Panayia Tinou* made no mention of such a place, and neither did the touristic notes on the map of Tinos that I had picked up in Chora. The name, however, had such a fascinating ring of archaic authenticity to it that as I repeated it to myself it wiped away any lingering doubt I had about missing Falatados and Steni.

Not even Dr. Christofilopoulos, with his summer home on Tinos, knew about or was in any way prepared for the geological oddity of Volax. A considerable expanse of gently hilly land spreads all around the village and is splotched with apparently exogenous boulders of various sizes. These boulders frequently are piled together so tightly that they appear to have shaped each other while coming to a halt eons ago. I felt this extraordinary scene could have animated the ancient myth explaining that the Archipelago came

6

into existence when Cronus emptied the remains of his bag of rocks into the Aegean after having created the continents. But I hardly had time to enjoy the intoxication of that notion before Andoni, who was old enough to remember the early Hollywood westerns, brought me back to my own era with his dead-on observation that the boulders would make a perfect set for a cowboy shootout.

Other Tinians in the meantime had driven up to Volax for Sunday lunch at the village *taverna*. We were lucky to get a couple of tables on the veranda after we returned from our exploration. Andoni disappeared inside, and no sooner did he return than our table was being covered with plates of roast kid, stewed Tinian baby beef, small cheese pies, three distinctly local kinds of cheese, mountain greens and green beans. "We are," said Andoni, unable this once to retrieve the English equivalent, "*koilodouloi*" – belly slaves. But he confessed this shamelessly as he and his wife smiled broadly and speared morsels of kid. The rest of us lost no time in following suit.

Dionysus the Wine-god was present in two species at our meal. He first joined us when the green beans were set down on the table. Actually called 'vine-beans' (*ambelofasoula*), the green beans are grown among grapevines and are recognizable by their very slim pods that bulge with tender seeds like a decade of rosary beads. This habit of Tinian winegrowing culture recalls the remote times when Dionysus was still a god of trees and annual vegetation. Even during late antiquity the fig tree was still attributed to Dionysus, and haricot beans were accorded a symbolic place of honor along with figs on the grand tables of the Greeks.

A flask of what I believe Homer would have described as "sparkling ruddy wine" was also brought to us. "This is from Volax," Andoni assured me. "We're making it on Tinos from a long time ago." The wine was called *koumariano*, after the grape from which it was made, whose name bore that of the neighboring village of Koumaros. I tasted the wine, a slightly sweet one, and did not doubt its pedigree. Nor had I ever come across any wine quite like it, not even on nearby islands. I was so pleased by this rare manifestation of Dionysus that I could have declared the day a triumph right then and spent the rest of it self-satisfied on the beach by the Aeolos Bay. I should have suspected the road to "pre-history" would be longer than that.

We descended from Volax into 'one hundred of one-hundred percent' agricultural country. The vegetation by that time of summer was mostly dried to a brownish straw color, with only occasional outcroppings of green on terraces where fruit trees or vines were growing and in the low-lying tract of olive groves running in from the bay of Kolymbithra on the northern coast. The landscape was dotted with the elaborately designed, trademark Venetian era Tinian dovecots, whose inhabitants in the dicey times of centuries past had been a source of meat.

I expected that we would wind up the excursion after we had climbed again and reached Andoni's native village of Aetofolia (Eagle's Nest), if only because the asphalt road gave out there. But instead, we just continued forward along an unpaved road leading into the mountains behind the village's perch. When that road ended, we kept going on a Michelin's nightmare of a roadbed that caused Rambo to hunker down in the back of the pickup and just roll with the punches. Adding to our discomfort, Dr. Christofilopoulos made a wrong turn that placed us in an extremely tight cul-de-sac. Nothing but chasm could be seen out the windshield as he twisted us back onto course. "Just think," said Babis, sitting in front and craning his neck towards me in the back rather than look out, "a week ago we were behind our desks in Washington." I was glad I had paid my respects at the icon.

I have no very exact idea about the location of the site where we ended up. We came to a stop down a long and narrow bypath past three makeshift gateways, each camouflaged with portable bushes as though the place were threatened by squatters. We were just below the end of a mountain spur that faces northeastward out to the Aegean. Andoni said we were where the "border" between Catholic and Orthodox lands had once been. I asked if the locale had a name and he answered Svilani, but I have looked for it in vain even on detailed maps of Tinos.

Below us were terraces that Andoni had inherited. He gave me, Babis and Dr. Christofilopoulos a climbing tour while his wife and sister went to collect zucchini and mountain oregano for the Aeolos Bay kitchen. Rambo trailed us at a distance and consistently took the less strenuous long way around the terraces rather than jump from one level to another, which prompted Andoni to remark that a change to a humbler name was in order for his mutt.

The mountain slopes we had seen since leaving Aetofolia were covered with abandoned terraces, and Andoni's cascade of them had not been tended carefully since his father's death. Vines were growing in untamed profusion on some of them. Andoni pointed out to us the vines that could be used for wine and the ones that were for table grapes and provided the best leaves for curing and, ultimately, stuffed grapevine leaves. He said he hoped to restore the terraces and the vines but that he did not have much time for the project in between tourist seasons. His son, he added, did not want so much as to see the place. It would seem that even the route to Svilani is destined to be forgotten.

At the end of one terrace stood an austere rectangular pillbox constructed from rough-hewn but tightly fitted small slabs of blackish stone. It was the drabbest, darkest Aegean structure I have ever seen. "Prehistory," proclaimed Andoni. Surely it was an architectural design from the year of 1, anyway. But the eye-opening signs of age-old ways were inside, where we saw the rudimentary facilities and implements Andoni's ancestors had for making wine. Even the furnishings – table, seats, bunk – were of the same stone as that used for the structure itself. It was as if we had been brought into Circe's dwelling. And when we went outside again and Andoni, surveying the Aegean and the sky, said, "Only you and God here," I felt he was slighting Homer's ghost.

2

ODD MEN OUT

"How you like the Batsi? We have sea, sand, clubs. Of course, is no Miami Beach." As he spoke, Zack, the operator of the modest rooms where my daughter and I were to stay on Andros for a week, was clearing away the remains of the continental breakfast we ate on the communal patio fronting the beach our first morning. I handed him my still half-full glass of bracingly acidic orange juice. "You no like the orange juice?" Zack continued. "I put the *lemoni* in it. (I remembered that lemons abound on Andros.) Is no fresh orange juice. People from Athens is say needs more sour, so I put the *lemoni*. You no like, tomorrow I no put for you."

I was surprised that Zack was taking a sounding of our reaction to Batsi so soon after our arrival. We had only arrived on Andros the night before. I laughed off the mention of Miami in the hope of convincing Zack that luxury was not what we were after. He evidently figured Miami would be an American's natural point of reference for judging beach vacation spots. He had seen the real place after all, not just old television shows filmed there. Andros is the preeminent Greek island of ship owners and seafarers, and Zack, like many other Andrians we would encounter, had been a merchant seaman and a frequent visitor to U.S. ports, Miami among them.

Aegean Islands

I was being more optimistic than frank about Batsi. We had come by ferry from the Attic port of Rafina on a Friday night and it seemed to us that the weekend crowd from Athens that came with us was stretching Batsi's Cycladic charm to the limit. It was in any case an abruptly assembled charm that did not bear any closer scrutiny than does the glitz of Miami Beach. The most positive thought we were having about Batsi that morning was that it beat Gavrion, the main ferry port ten minutes up the coast, where we had landed.

Within half an hour of chatting with Zack we were on a bus out of town seeking a less agitated Andros. We found a dead standstill early in the afternoon at Menites, a shady mountain village along the fruitful vale of Messaria at mid-island. Menites was the ideal setting for a relaxing lunch, and the only other customer at the *taverna* where we ate it was a fisherman seated one table over from us enjoying a beer. He gave us a summary account of the fish caught off Andros. The best fish, he said, is one called *skathari*, but it is rare and usually taken home by the fishermen or given to good friends, not sold – thus a rather academic catch whose English name was not worth rummaging for as far as I was concerned. But whether or not any fish were available in the *taverna*'s kitchen, the proprietor's mother, who was doing the cooking, made only one recommendation, *froutalia*, Andros's mint-strewn cross between an ancient Greek omelet and a medieval Venetian *frittata*, with a post-Columbian addition of potatoes for good measure.

The *taverna*-keeper remarked, with feigned incredulity, on our carrying bottled water on Andros, whose original name, Hydroussa, aptly alluded to the island's many springs. He pointed out a battery of spouts twenty meters up the road where we could refill the bottle with absolutely fresh water. The spring of Menites anciently was sacred to Dionysus and ran with the god's own vintage on the occasion of his annual feast. His divine powers obviously were in first gush back then. I had to wash the *froutalia* down with a golden yellow elixir trampled out by none other than the proprietor.

We walked beyond the spouts and around the village after lunch. There were a lot of lemon trees, but lemons were laying uncollected all about the ground around them as if agriculture were a tertiary activity trailing navigation and tourism by a country mile – or else nobody but Zack had much use for *lemoni*.

A taxi-driver who was snoozing in his cab in the shade of several lemon trees opened his eyes upon hearing us and I asked him whether he could take us back to Batsi. He said he had an appointment to pick up a fare down the road in a quarter-of-an-hour for a ride to Gavrion to catch a ferry, but that there might be room for us. The passenger turned out to be a lone elderly man who did not at all mind sharing the cab with us. Both the driver and the passenger were ex-seamen, and most of their conversation along the way consisted of a comparison of information about shipping lines and vessels, with frequent casual mention of the well-known Andrian shipping families. Occasionally they would break off into broken English to share with us some random memory of their travels along the East, West or Gulf coasts.

Menites had been a tempting taste of Andros and as we approached Batsi I could read in my daughter's expression my own discontent with our home port. That evening, after being engulfed by the multitude exiting 'Forrest Gump' at the open-air movie theater, I knew we would have to hoist anchor the very next day if we were to last a week on Andros. In the morning I had my daughter pack a duffel bag with clothing and toiletries sufficient for three days, and we caught the first bus to the main town of Chora, or Andros, on the eastern coast of the island beyond Menites.

Chora immediately had a different feel about it than Batsi, a sense of being itself, of being the place the natives really want it to be. This difference is heavily bankrolled, as the Chorans collectively own a significant chunk of the world's commercial maritime fleet. The negative side of Chora from our peripatetic perspective was that when the Chorans flock back to their place of origin each summer, after spending the rest of the year in distant places like New York and New Jersey, it is in the expectation of spending time among their own kind: If the town does not dance to the tourists' tune, neither does it make many bunks available to them.

In the uncertainty of the moment I decided on a non-budgeted splurge at the Hotel Pighi Sariza, the only hostelry on Andros that might give Miami a run for the money. The hotel was, however, a mountain retreat, not a beach resort, being located ten minutes inland from Chora by taxi in the village of Apikia. Its location was owing to the Sariza spring (*pighi*), which is the source of the most widely known bottled water in Greece. The water is bottled in a plant next door to the hotel.

We were greeted at the Pighi Sariza by the desk clerk with whom I had spoken by phone from Chora to engage a room. He glanced at the data in my passport and, noticing my birthplace, congratulated me as "a fellow New Yorker." I expressed surprise because of his accent, which was not American, and he explained that he was a U.S. citizen and had been living in New York. He righteously emphasized that he had never been a Greek citizen – he had not been born in Greece and only his mother was Greek – and that he was in Greece now only to fulfill the Greek legal requirement that, as a non-citizen, he work there for three years in order to take possession of his mother's estate. He was not happy to be an indentured servant in Greece, and he lamented the Byzantine behavior of the Greeks ("Nobody shoots from the hip here.").

Aegean Islands

Oddly, luggage and personal items were laying about the room we were given. We returned to the reception desk to inform the clerk, and he consulted a woman who had also been behind the counter previously. In the meantime a burly little bearded man came to the counter. He had glasses strung round his neck and papers in his hand, and I would have thought him a delivery person with invoices to be signed had he not joined in the discussion about our room assignment. He recommended that the luggage be removed and the room given to us since the other party was to have checked out. But the woman wanted to tolerate the late departure and give us a different room. At this point the mix-up over the room became fodder for a squabble between the woman and the bearded man, and it was apparent that they were the husband and wife operators of Hotel Pighi Sariza. The woman capped her argument by coolly firing a broadside, "I watch out for the customers, not like you." Her husband instantly ignited in a rage and rampaged around the spacious lobby and balcony area for a minute or two before exiting onto the terrace. The clerk took it all in stride and gave us the key to a vacant room.

Mini-bus transportation from Pighi Sariza to nearby beaches was at our disposal and we requested this service late that afternoon. It was the volatile owner himself, Manousos by name, who drove us down to the beach at Stenies, a village close to Chora and second only to it worldwide in terms of dead-weight tonnage per capita. Along the way he related the story behind his hotel. He had been moved to build it by what he described virtually as a mystical attraction for the Sariza spring. Working like a demon, sleeping and eating irregularly, he had the entire facility up and running in just eight months. Before the hotel project, Manousos had been a seaman. (While exploring Pighi Sariza earlier, I had wondered at the plethora of eclectic decorations and knickknacks scattered about in its public rooms. It was almost embarrassing to recognize items that I myself had either bought for a pittance or passed up for good sense years earlier in places separated by as many meridians of longitude as the Black and South China seas.)

For all I know Manousos may have shared in the erratic and irascible nature of the Greek gods. My daughter, however, believed him mortally plagued by faulty electrical wiring. She was convinced of it fifteen minutes after Manousos was to have picked us up from the beach at Stenies – she was sure he had forgotten about us. I held out another fifteen minutes in favor of an explanation that allowed for a Levantine time frame. But when I called Pighi Sariza at that time Manousos answered and candidly blurted that we had in fact slipped his mind. As a demonstration of his goodwill toward us – or else to ward off my daughter's evil eye – he stopped off at a bakery in Chora after picking us up and treated us to *kalsounia*, the local confection of nuts and honey. That there was nothing personal about Manousos's neglect was clear when he subsequently pulled up to a greengrocer's for two crates of *horta*, or wild greens, and apologized abjectly for causing the man to keep the shop open late (the grocer, as if hearing all of it for the hundredth time, waved Manousos off silently with the back of his hand and double-timed in closing up).

Upon our return to Pighi Sariza the clerk delayed us at the desk and was at pains to explain the earlier mix-up about our room. He said that when he took my telephone call that morning he thought I was another Miles Lambert who had called several days earlier to make a reservation for the coming week. The clerk had assigned this person to the room he had first sent us to, and he showed us a phone memo reservation slip with the name Miles Lambert and the indication of the room number on it. My daughter and I had not expected any explanation about the room but we were astonished by the uncanny coincidence of names and travel plans and looked forward to meeting my alter ego.

Our great delight at Pighi Sariza was in the meals. Indeed, only the availability of *skathari* could possibly have added anything more to the experience. Our waiter, who went by the name Lefty, was from Athens, not Andros, and he was a polished server. He was always solicitous in helping us choose from the menu, though perhaps overzealous in not telling us about dishes, such as *horta* with fresh capers, that he assumed Americans would not like. Lefty's motives sometimes were obscure. For instance I would have liked to express our appreciation to the chef personally for the meals, but Lefty did not think this could or should be arranged as the chef was "a very mixed up person." Lefty made no bones about his disgruntlement at Pighi Sariza, and he could hardly wait for his one-season contract with Manousos to end. Lefty advised us in no uncertain terms that his employer was "a madman." (My daughter was so thoroughly spooked about Manousos after listening to Lefty unburden himself, that she would have given credence to tales of axe murders at the hotel.)

The afternoon before we checked out of Pighi Sariza I stopped at the desk to ask about my namesake, the other Miles Lambert, who was supposed to have arrived that day. "He never showed up," the clerk responded. "That happens sometimes." I gave the matter no more conscious thought that day, but it occurred to me spontaneously as I was waking up the next morning that the clerk had concocted the whole story as a face-saving ruse to camouflage his slipup in assigning us to an occupied room. Did he imagine, in a fit of self-importance, that I was going to denounce him to the local tourism authorities? And would his inheritance then be at risk? It was all too Byzantine for a trueborn New Yorker to contemplate.

We had wanted to reach some of the villages of northern Andros while at Pighi Sariza, but we did not manage it. Our interest was that the patois in the north is a medieval Albanian dialect, not Greek. The day after leaving Pighi Sariza we were in a *taverna* in Gavrion for lunch and we thought our waiter might be from the north because he looked so different from the other Andrians we met. But on closer observation it was apparent that he was no clodhopper from some remote village; and my daughter remarked that he was more in tune with the subtleties of Western leisure fashion than anyone else she had noticed among the inhabitants. He also demonstrated a sophisticated turn of mind when I asked him about the wine on tap. At first he said it was from Andros, but a few minutes later he came back and said it was actually from the mainland. He apologized for having fibbed and said he thought I was joking when I asked where it came from.

Once things were on the level we had a friendly conversation with the waiter. He told us something of his own origin, which turned out to be from the town of Xanthi in northeastern mainland Greece. He had come to Andros some years previously with his wife, who also had no roots there. Naturally I went ahead and asked what brought them to the island. At that question a dark look came over his face and he clammed up as if he had previously led a life of crime and was laying low on Andros under an assumed identity. I did not pursue my line of questioning. This was partly out of sympathy for the waiter … and partly because we were still at sea trying to sort out the crew at Pighi Sariza and did not need more to puzzle about.

Greek Salad

We had always intended to return to Batsi. We had never even relinquished our room at Zack's because it was too inexpensive not to 'insure' our accommodations for when we returned to that side of the island. But I had not told Zack beforehand about our field trip to eastern Andros lest he think I was longing for Miami Beach. He noticed our absence, though, and it apparently cost me my credibility with him, as if we had been AWOL. I think so because on the day we checked out Zack behaved as though he doubted we were really leaving Andros. He had a friend of his take all three of us to Gavrion by car; he stood at the door of the travel agency as if blocking our retreat while we bought our tickets; and he waited with us until the ferry came and we went aboard.

As we milled around with him in Gavrion, Zack reminisced about the States: "I love the apple pie. Always I was order apple pie. With ice cream – à la mode. Three balls ice cream. And with a big glass-a-milk." I realized too late that this was not a man to be trifled with.

3

OUT OF MY DEPTH

Syros had long stuck in my craw. A dozen years before I visited I had a conversation with a Syran dining room steward on an Aegean ferry and he intrigued me when he mentioned a "Catholic hill" and an "Orthodox hill" at Ermoupolis, the island's port and capital. The next year, while returning to the mainland from deeper in the Cyclades, I actually did purchase a ticket for Syros. But a hard rain was falling and the hour was late as we approached the harbor, and the part of Ermoupolis that could be seen from on deck looked scruffy and without much Cycladic allure. After an unfervent gander at the two denominational hills I quickly went and paid the additional passage back to Piraeus. Missing Syros never sat well with me, though. I always had the nagging feeling that I might have been too hasty in trading in my ticket.

I do not mean to leave the impression that I could regret my reception when I finally did disembark at Ermoupolis. Had I visited on the earlier occasion I would have been just another arrival off a ferry. I would have had to fend for myself and rely on my usual modus operandi in making the acquaintance of the inhabitants. Instead, waiting for me with mini-van and driver on the quay was John Vatis, a Syran shipping magnate. I would want for neither comfort nor companionship while on Syros.

Greek Salad

John (he had lived in the United States for twenty-five years and used this name) had established a vineyard and winery on his Syros estate. He and his wife, Helen, divided their time between Athens and Syros and spent the warm months and growing season on the island. John had wanted to play the complete host and put me up at the estate, which originally had been a minuscule monastery (of the Orthodox kind) and thus had a number of serviceable cells. But that summer it was extremely difficult to find local help for seasonal housework. The Vatises finally resorted to the recent pan-Hellenic solution and engaged Filipinos. A man and a woman were hired, but they had been summarily released on the spot when John and Helen discovered them embraced on the carpeting one day shortly before my arrival. A secondary consequence was that John had to reserve a room for me half an hour away in the coastal village of Finikas.

We took a leisurely and roundabout route from Ermoupolis to Finikas so John could show me the vineyards of two friends of his who were growing grapes for his wine. The inviting hills and lowlands of southern Syros were in complete contrast to the drab and unwelcoming mountains of the north that provide the first impression of the island when arriving by ferry from Piraeus. I was ready to give credence to Homer's description of a Syros once rich in grain and wine. John said commercial agriculture was practically extinct on the island by the time of the Second World War and had only recently been on the upswing. Shipyards and textile plants formerly had made Syros the most highly industrialized island of the Aegean. In the shaded seaside village of Dellagrazia that we passed through just before reaching Finikas, John called my attention to the numerous old summer manses of the island elite. In the middle of the village stood Greece's oldest country club, founded by Syran captains of industry around 1905.

Dellagrazia's full and original name is Madonna della Grazia, a remnant from Venetian times. I nevertheless did a double take when I saw a Catholic nun at work in the kitchen of the hotel in Finikas a few minutes later. I asked John about the religious split on the island and he surprised me with the statistics that Syros as a whole is one-half Catholic and that its rural part is four-fifths Catholic. The Venetian influence on religion had been so strong that the island had few Orthodox inhabitants until accepting a massive influx of Chian and other Aegean refugees from the Turks in the early 19th century, during the Greek war for independence. John admitted a preference to have Syran Catholics as the year-round caretakers of his estate despite his and Helen's Orthodox adhesion. His preference for them was based on what he said was their wider world view that had been inculcated for generations by priests trained in western Europe. (The wife of the hotel's owner, however, must have had a more 'parochial' education because when I asked her about the Catholic Greek newspaper on her desk she asked in all earnestness whether there are Catholics in Washington.)

After assuring my comfort in the hotel, John invited me to join him and Helen for a swim in the bay at Finikas later in the afternoon. I accepted and later on decided to await them on the strand of beach directly across the street from the hotel in order to sample the water in the meantime. But when they pulled up in the van, which was piloted by a different driver than before, they were smiling genially at my assumption and said that what they had in mind was to take me out to their yacht moored in the bay. They had rethought the situation as soon as they had seen me, however. They told me to stay put and that they would send a motor launch to shore for me. Helen would have none of my readiness to trouble myself by gathering up my things at once and hopping into the van. She insisted on my ease and a beachside retrieval by boat.

Aboard the yacht, I was offered a choice of aquatic activities: water skiing, scuba diving or raft paddling. Just to be a sport I paddled a few great circles in the bay. I was encouraged to make it a triathlon experience, but I did not want to demonstrate my lack of accomplishment (where I was raised, keeping one's head above water was attainment enough in life). I turned my paddle in and dried off, and John handed me a copy of the *International Herald-Tribune* while apologizing for the circumstance that the paper unavoidably arrives a day late on Syros. But being more anxious to yap about John's wine – and knowing that time, events and the Dow-Jones Average are not of the essence to my social class – I only looked the pages over politely and cursorily.

The difference between John's lifestyle and mine became all too apparent as he spoke about how he became involved with wine. The story began when he moved back to Greece in the 1970s and bought a summer home on Hydra. Once while on a sailing trip from Hydra he moored at his native Syros. Alongside came another yacht bearing the widow of the industrialist who had bought John's grandfather's Syros estate during the Second World War. She asked John to buy it back, and he, not pleased with trends on Hydra and full of fond memories of youthful summers spent on his grandfather's property, agreed without a second thought. At first he planted some vines just for his own needs. But after doctors told him that his time on deck had brought him to the verge of serious skin cancer, he had to find an avocation other than sailing and so decided to upgrade his interest in wine. Money being no object, he had new terraces built and expanded his vineyard four-fold.

For the evening, I was invited to a supper party John and Helen were giving at a *taverna* in Finikas. The place was so close to the hotel that I could have walked to it in a few minutes' time, but my hosts came with a car and yet a third driver and drove me there.

Greek Salad

The *taverna* looked like someone's home, and our group took up practically the entire porch even though there were only ten of us. The three semi-retired sisters who owned the place were cooking mostly on special request by old friends like John. The whole supper consisted of the sisters' hors d'oeuvres, of which John was particularly fond. Great platters of these substantial Greek *mezethes* were placed before us, and they were replaced several times. For my part I could hardly stop eating the potato-and-cheese croquettes.

John's wine, a white one, shined against the fare and enlivened the conversation. Most of the table talk, however, was considerably beyond my petty experience of life. Two topics that really put me in my place were the purchase of a personal jet airplane and the creation of a family-funded Syran ethnographical museum. Unable to contribute anything to such discussions, I reminded myself of the ancient advice of Simonides, who said he had "never been sorry for having kept silent, but many a time for having spoken." When the prospective purchaser of the airplane caught my eye while talking about the merits of a particular type of jet, I just looked away quickly and took a few more potato balls. The only person in my own league was John's local CPA, a lapsed Syran Catholic and practicing bon vivant about whom the others worried at parting time, several hours later, lest he careen off somewhere on his motor scooter (he had demolished his car after a recent revelry).

Aegean Islands

Driver Number Three picked me up the next morning and brought me to the Vatis estate for the meat of my visit, the vineyard and cellar tour. The estate, called Ayia Paraskevi after the small church and former monastery complex, was situated on a parched mountainside and had a commanding view eastward over Ermoupolis and the harbor. A fleet of vehicles was arrayed under cover by the entrance to the property, and off to one side could be seen the helicopter pad that John and Helen needed before Syros had an airport.

John was waiting for me in the main residence. With him was his enologist, who had flown in from Athens on the early morning flight. We first went into the vineyard terraces, where John commented that he was "cultivating under Israeli conditions – no water and very bad land." Then he showed me the elaborate drip-irrigation system that had been installed to counteract the environment, and at the cellar I saw all the latest enological paraphernalia needed to bring desert wine up to snuff. The enologist was especially delighted to have a new Italian pump that moved the grape mass from the crusher to the press through a hose without the wine-stuff ever touching any part of the pump itself. He said the apparatus worked on what he characterized as "the principle of the toothpaste tube," and he jumped up and down on the hose several times to elucidate the principle. We also tasted wines, of which the curiosity was a 5-year-old chardonnay. John had acquired a taste for chardonnay while living

Greek Salad

in California and planted that variety along with Aegean sorts of grapes when he put in his vineyard.

Lunch was served on the terrace of the residence. Helen's mother had prepared a *pastitsio* of a quality above what even an inveterately hopeful fan of Greek dishes might imagine *pastitsio* has in it, and of course a bottle of John's wine (appropriately, the Aegean type) was opened to do it justice. As we ate, John related the history of the Ayia Paraskevi complex, which was built to commemorate the daughter of a prominent family. The girl had just married and together with her new husband was killed by the freak explosion of their vessel off Hydra while on their honeymoon cruise in the mid-19th century. Her family later bequeathed the property to the (Orthodox) Archbishop of Syros, who in turn left it to his grandnephew, John's grandfather. It occurred to me somewhere into my second glass of *Vatis* that the tragic tale had possibilities – now that the vine was growing on the estate – for a metaphor on death and transformation which would not be lost on either a medieval troubadour or a modern wine scribe.

In the evening came a social engagement in Ermoupolis. Driver Number Three came to fetch me at Finikas and brought me back to Ayia Paraskevi to pick up John. (Driver Number Two would bring Helen later.) Down in town we drove up to a recently refurbished hotel at the harbor so that John, who was hosting the dinner, could check on arrangements. We had time to kill afterward and John used it to give me his signature tour of Ermoupolis. Not far from the hotel was the once exclusive Vaporia (Steamships) quarter that had been the town's Captain's Row. John pointed out his birthplace there. We also passed the old theater, which had been erected by the European oriented elite of Syros several decades before they turned to their country club project at Dellagrazia. The theater was in the process of being renovated in connection with the resurrection of the tradition of a Syran symphony season. John was donating the seats.

We also stopped across from an obscure and tight passageway between two buildings that housed government offices. John wanted me to see where the official temperature readings for Syros are taken. He had sent the temperature data to an enologist in California who wrote back saying that Syros has great temperatures for vacations but not for chardonnay. But that was before the enologist visited Ayia Paraskevi at John's invitation the following summer and found himself needing a jacket on the veranda in the evening – and before John discovered that the temperature readings were taken in the daytime in a stuffy nook downtown.

The occasion for the hotel dinner was a visit to Syros by the Governor of the Aegean Islands, whose seat is at Rhodes. I knew the dinner was going to be more formal than the previous evening's as soon as John suggested that I wear slacks rather than the shorts

Greek Salad

I wore to the *taverna* in Finikas. And indeed the meal was served in courses.

About twenty people were present and I was careful to sit toward the junior end of the table, where my chief companions in small talk were a fashion-shop owner, his dentist wife (the state of teeth on Syros, she said, was "horrible," apparently for lack of any principle of the toothpaste tube), and again John's CPA. Another case or more of John's wine was consumed and several persons again expressed concern about the CPA's drive home (I did not wonder, because during the dessert course he had occasion to mention the time, when he still had his car, that he leveled a kiosk in Ermoupolis with it).

A car and Driver Number One were put at my disposal the next day for touring of my choice. I had him take me to the 13th century enclave of Ano (Upper) Syros, which is the "Catholic hill." Although it adjoins Ermoupolis, Ano Syros actually is a separate communal entity and also centuries older than the capital, which sprang to life only with the influx of refugees in the 19th century. We parked outside a medieval gateway and proceeded on foot from there up to the ancient church of Ayios Georgios, otherwise known as San Giorgio, at the top of Ano Syros. This strained our navigational instincts as well as our stamina. We were nearly out of wind when a remarkably stocky denizen who took up half the width of the lane gave us directions and encouragement ("If you've got feet, you'll make it. Don't fear."). Our reward for our trouble was a panoramic inland view that took in John's Ayia Paraskevi estate as well.

John came to Finikas with Driver Number Three and the van the following morning to take me to the ferry. Arriving early in Ermoupolis, we drove past the ferry quay and onto the pier that extended beyond the hotel where the dinner for the Governor of the Aegean had been. John was going to show me the small maritime academy, which he referred to as "the King's Point of Greece." Two men were on the pier and the one nudged the other to point out John. It occurred to me that never in my Aegean travels did I have so little contact with ordinary people as on Syros. John, meanwhile, had noticed the cargo vessel moored at the end of the pier. "I almost bought that ship," he said. From his amused tone I could have thought he was talking about a mere yacht.

4

IN SEARCH OF TRADITION

"I'll change your mood on Paros and on Naxos." The bright promise of these words to a Cycladic tune influenced me one morning in Piraeus while I was mulling over the day's sailing schedule. The one name sounded as pretty as the other, and my choice in favor of Paros came down to the fact that an 'appellation of origin' had recently been authorized for a dry red wine made there. Naxos, having no official standing in wine, had no special appeal to the wine enthusiast in me; its advantage was with opera buffs.

I value the scope for spontaneity in choosing Aegean ports of call. I have never, for instance, reserved rooms ahead when traveling by myself in case I am moved to change my mind. This policy has never landed me on the beach for the night, but I did have some second thoughts about it on Paros. I was in need of fuel as well as orientation when the ferry arrived at the port of Parikia, and my eye fixed on the cheery façade and jaunty awning of the Aligaria *taverna* almost as soon as I was ashore. I liked the look of the dishes inside, and stayed. I was the last customer for lunch, save one. I preceded by several minutes an expatriate Mytilinian who was engaged in the Parian tourist trade. He took a personal interest in me the moment he noticed my suitcase on the floor next to my table, and while we ate he cast his net of palaver from across the tables separating us.

I could not reconcile the image of a Mytilinian beating the drum for Paros as much as this agent did. I was even more wary when he tried to hand me off to his younger brother who had popped his head in the door and spotted him. Nonetheless I was so intrigued by the flow of events up to this point that I played my part and briefly left with the sibling understudy when he said he could show me a bargain room nearby. But the room proved to be at rock bottom of the budget category. I could only conclude that the brothers must have fled Mytilini owing to some touristic disgrace they had brought upon their native island.

On my return to the Aligaria the elder brother immediately sensed his mistake in judging my wallet for lodgings by my choice in eateries and assured me that I could indeed have a room in a real hotel. I was snared when on top of that he said he would arrange to have the president of the island wine growers' cooperative come to meet me at the hotel.

The co-op president came over that same afternoon shortly after the midday rest. We spoke mostly about the tradition of red wine on Paros and how the island landed an appellation of origin entitlement. I had noticed a bottled *retsina* from the co-op at the Aligaria but did not raise it as a topic with the president since producers throughout Greece resinate some white wine so as to tap the market created by tourists who ply the Aegean oblivious to local wine traditions and order *retsina* wherever they go. I was sure I had a firm grasp on tradition in this case because James Bent, a 19th century authority on the Cyclades, wrote that he had found *retsina* only on Kythnos among that island group. I also thought that if *retsina* were integral to Parian wine tradition it would have been mentioned in that vein by the co-op president, who was about sixty, or old enough to know a thing or two about local traditions. But he had passed right over *retsina*.

A subsequent stroll through Parikia soon put me on its outskirts, on a road paralleling the mountainous ridge at the town's back. I came across a man working with his toddling granddaughter beside him in a vineyard parcel adjacent to the road. After we chatted a while about the kinds of grapes he was cultivating he invited me to sample his wines in the small ground-level wine cellar he had there. Inside the cellar so many mosquitoes were flitting about that I was reminded of a comment by one of Plutarch's drinking buddies: "why, spurning the fine bouquet of mellow wine like this, do we not drink coarse, inferior wine out of the cask – wine surrounded by a choir of singing mosquitoes" (*Table-talk*). I wondered what my taste-buds might be in for.

The wine grower handed me two glasses, both of them filled halfway with wine of the very palest discernibly orange color, even incipiently pinkish, though short of the so called partridge-eye and swan-eye shades preferred in some cosmopolitan markets. I was able to tell, despite the interferences run on my senses by the mosquitoes, that one of the two wines was resinated. But this reassuring confirmation of my tasting prowess did nothing to help me overcome the perplexity I felt in having uncovered a *retsina* not in a commercial winery, but in a farmer's shack. I was all the more troubled because it was good *retsina*. I thought the Parians must have known for some time what they are about when it comes to resinating wine. Less cocky now about my knowledge of Cycladic tradition, I asked somewhat anxiously whether *retsina* is "a traditional wine" on Paros. The wine grower, who seemed to be around sixty-five and about as acquainted with local tradition as anyone might be, replied that it is. 'Singing mosquitoes' indeed. This buzzing question was not going to leave me alone now.

The owner-cook of the Aligaria had recommended that I speak with Georges Moussa, a Frenchman who was residing just up the lane from the *taverna*. I found the house early that evening, and Georges and I went to the Aligaria to talk further about the island over a bottle of Parian red wine. Georges had been living on Paros with his wife and two children for five years after having left the French diplomatic service because of an accumulation of general dissatisfaction and unfulfillment. The family had not regretted the change of lifestyle, except occasionally in the summer when a certain sort of young vagabond, testing the legendary Greek hospitality to its limits, will barge into a home and ask for beer, wine or *ouzo*.

Georges had used his time on Paros to write a book each on that island and neighboring Sifnos and had become something of an authority on them. In talking about the island wines he made no mention of resin at all until he recommended that I go to Sifnos. Georges said that at the humble O Manganas *taverna* in Artemona on Sifnos I would find a true master of the rotisserie who serves his own "excellent" *retsina*. I was once more caught off guard. Sifnos was known to me as being nothing if not traditional. What was I to do but check out Georges's story?

The boat that took me to Sifnos should have been named Tantalus. Although the island appeared to lie little more than an hour away, this boat was only able to inch its way across the water, no matter that she was piloted by a heavy-bearded Poseidon in overalls and Greek fisherman's cap. The crossing took nearly three hours. And as the Tantalus chugged along, visions of Sifnian cooks began to dance in my head. I made straight for a *taverna* along the quay at the port of Kamares when we finally arrived and was served an outstanding dish of calamari in dark wine sauce plus a measure of the house's own Sifnian wine … a *retsina*.

Aegean Islands

I did not hang around Kamares but instead took a bus to my ultimate destination, inland Artemona. The village was unusual for its many elegant homes. They had been built by wealthy Sifnians or their descendants who had been expelled from Egypt along with other foreign nationals by Abdul Nasser in the 1950s. Artemona also harbored a more insular and traditional element, however. These persons, the locals proper, could be spotted by dress and speech that lacked any cosmopolitan polish. That day they all seemed to be remarking on the Easter slaughter of lambs which was in progress. From the great anticipation in their voices I could sense them licking their chops after forty days of meatless fasting.

O Manganas that evening lived up to Georges's billing. Worthy *retsina* from the family cellar was being poured to accompany spitted lamb fit for any old Mouton-Rothschild. The only sour note came when I interrogated the proprietor's father about the *retsina* and he assured me that it is "traditional" on Sifnos. What could I say? The old boy was in his seventies and a local through and through. Maybe resinated wine gained its cloven foothold at the expense of tarring, another antique practice for preserving wine, whose advantage must have been in its application to odoriferous goatskin wine sacks. In tramping along the ovine paths around Artemona I could imagine that goatskins and tarring were not much farther back in its past than the arrival of the Nasser refugees.

Greek Salad

I reported back to Georges when I returned to Paros the next day. He now suggested that I look up a certain Nikos Pantelaios in the mountain village of Lefkes in the interior of the island. Georges told me that Lefkes was reputed to have the best vineyards on Paros, although not many any longer, and that Pantelaios usually had a small surplus of wine for sale. More particularly, Georges thought I should taste Pantelaios's semi-sweet red wine. So did I when Georges said that such wine is Paros's "traditional" specialty.

I arrived in Lefkes about midday on Good Friday to the sound of a priest's chant blaring over the village from loudspeakers set atop the church. Most of the inhabitants must have been inside the church because very few people were to be seen in the village itself. However, I did encounter several souls from whom to inquire about finding Pantelaios. I quickly got the idea that Pantelaios was a common family name in Lefkes and that my quarry was the entrepreneur of the place, since each of those whom I asked had to think the matter over and answered along the lines of, "Oh, you must mean the tailor." At length I learned that Pantelaios-the-tailor-and-vintner was at church. He was selling the candles there.

It was an uneasy feeling to be entering the Lord's house with my mind fixed on worldly goods. And it abated only after I was well within, where the deep shadows and flickering candles did so much for the looks of some of the womenfolk that other lusts took hold of me. I was put even more at ease about my wine mission after Pantelaios was pointed out to me and I sized him up as a type who would not object to my approaching him in church about mundane affairs. Indeed he did not, and we agreed to meet at his shop in about an hour.

I took off into the vineyards above the village to pass the time until the rendezvous. Lefkes was a delight to look upon from the vantages there. Far from the village that Bent found "dirty and black in the extreme" a century earlier, Lefkes now fully lived up to its name, whose root is in the ancient Greek word for white. The village positively gleamed. And the view towards non-appellation Naxos was magnificent. I gloated as only a wine fetishist might.

Pantelaios's storefront was as plain as could be, but when he arrived and opened up I saw an interior which in its mercantile way was as ornately Byzantine as the church of Lefkes. It was a hole-in-the-wall crammed to the rafters with dry goods, hardware, wrappings, toys – in short, a true *pantopoleion*, or 'place selling all.' Because of Easter, candles at that time were literally all over the place, piled and hanging, underfoot and overhead. Daylight came sneaking in under the eaves of the doorway and cast into the center of the room a muted brightness that diminished in intensity towards the walls and had the effect of setting off the goods in an almost surrealistic way. I felt

Greek Salad

as though I understood perfectly the nature of each sort of material of which the things were made. Something similar must have happened for the three small children who came in from church with their mother and stood silently while slowly turning their heads in awe to take in every square inch of Pantelaios's place. FAO Schwartz would not have been more fascinating to them.

A neighbor brought in some shrimp, a permissible and valued Lenten protein food, that were straight off the grill. Pantelaios and I stood while picking them out of their slightly charred jackets and munching, and he told me all about Lefkes wine. Certain now of the wines I would be tasting, I allowed the merchant of Lefkes to show me his vinous wares without any cues from me. But out he came from behind his shop-keeper's iconostasis with a glass of … *retsina*. Flabbergasted, I glanced wistfully out the doorway in the direction of Naxos, the island I had spurned for the sake of Parian red wine. Looking back to Pantelaios, who appeared to be around forty-five and to have an acquaintance with local habits beyond his years, I asked him whether *retsina*, which he had not mentioned at all in our preceding discussion, is "traditional" in Lefkes. He answered that it is traditional, and I cringed each time he emitted the word *rekina*, for while I had not heard that pronunciation from other lips on Paros, I thought that such a dialectical corruption of *retsina*'s name surely must be evidence of a hoary habit of making resinated wine. It was with a bitterness born of feeling seriously misled by earlier explorers of the Aegean that I finally tasted the semi-sweet red wine of Lefkes.

I set out from Parikia the following day for the fishing and farming community of Naoussa on the northeastern coast. This time I was going on the rec-ommendation of a British excursionist I met on the boat to Sifnos. He had been sojourning in Naoussa and he told me of a good homemade red wine he had been buying there. But I failed to find the house dis-playing the 'Wine for Sale' sign that he said was posted outside, even though I had in hand a little map he had drawn for me. I stopped a local man for further directions, and much to my surprise he claimed to have wine of his own. We headed off to his shop together.

The elderly Naoussan impressed me as epitomiz-ing the virtues long attributed to Parians by their Cy-cladic neighbors. Parians are considered zealous only in their conscious pursuit of a 'measured' life, and they especially value politeness of demeanor and a concilia-tory frame of mind, all of which is said to reward them with a long life expectancy. As befitted him, the old man turned out to be a former mayor of his commu-nity. I felt absolutely certain of the purity of his roots in local tradition when he told me he makes the is-land's semi-sweet red wine. But of course a prudent Parian has the sense not to start a wine tasting with a wine like that. And this estimable fellow did have other wines to show me. He began with a glass of his ... *retsina*.

Perhaps encouraged by my host's consummately serene and forthright manner, I remained unflustered as I prepared to put my question yet again. "Is it," I asked, mustering my very best Greek pronunciation, "a traditional wine here?" The ex-mayor looked me straight in the eye and with all the authority in the world issued an unequivocal Yes. My head dropped in a whirlpool of exasperation. Just what, I wondered, could I believe from all the old books?

Then, in the pit of my dejection, I had the inspired idea to abandon my vocabulary of nebulous words like "traditional," which might have a very different connotation to an elderly Parian than to me. I looked up and asked simply, "Did your grandfathers make *retsina*?" "Oh, no," said the seventy-ish winemaker, who had known many a Parian grandfather. "*Retsina* is being made here for less than fifty years. Maybe we're doing it thirty years now."

5

AMONG OUR SOUVENIRS

We got home from Greece yesterday, and I've been sorting through the flotsam that accumulated haphazardly along our itinerary. Most of it comes from Naxos in the central Cyclades, and as I look at these few mementoes it's easy to relive our visit.

The business card of the Hotel Anixis

You can't travel the Aegean in summer with a 15-year-old daughter and two large suitcases and not have accommodations lined up. Two American college girls we met on Santorini had just been to Naxos and recommended the Anixis, in the main town of Naxos, or Chora, so I phoned ahead and booked a room.

The hotel's card is a folding one with four sides and boasts two full-color photos of the hotel, one showing the manager's father working in the garden. I'd gotten into a conversation with the old man before we'd even settled into our room. He told me about *kitro*, the Naxian liqueur distilled from the leaves of the citron tree, which used to be 'baked' in barrels set out in great rows extending back from the waterfront. During the Second World War, he told me, the Italians thought the barrels contained petroleum. "*Kitro* was the first victim of the bombing, and they reported to Mussolini that the mission was a success."

The Anixis was better than I'd hoped for, given the age of our informants. The glass shelf above the bathroom sink, however, was slippery when wet and sloped imperceptibly downward, away from the wall, which caused me the loss of a glass of good peasant wine that I'd bought in the village of Komiaki, when I set the glass down temporarily on the shelf. But what the Anixis lacked in amenities it more than made up for in its setting. Motor scooters cannot pass through the narrow lanes where the hotel is tucked away and mornings arrived with nothing but the sound of the waves crashing along the nearby coastline. This rare advantage in a bustling Aegean town merits touting in the blank space on the business card.

An anthology of old travel descriptions of Naxos

I bought this little book in Naxos town for late-night reading. The engraving on the cover shows the island's old Venetian fortress and the town below, as viewed from the remains of an ancient temple on an offshore rock now connected to the island by a short causeway.

My daughter and I climbed up the winding medieval lanes of the fortress, or Kastro, late one afternoon. The Kastro has remained an enclave of Catholic

Aegean Islands

Naxians ever since Venetian times. Alongside the Catholic church at the top of the Kastro is the former Catholic French school attended for two years in his youth by the Orthodox Cretan writer Nikos Kazantzakis, who ever remained phobic about Rome. Decades later, in his autobiographical *Return to Greco*, Kazantzakis claimed to remember every detail of the climb through the Kastro when his father took him up to enroll him. The trauma of a new school where people cross themselves backwards must sharpen a child's memory cells, because I'm hardly away from Naxos one week and already all I can remember is the grateful shade of the lone tree by the fountain beside the old school.

As for the ancient temple on the rock, all that remains is an entranceway, which has become the symbol of Naxos. The writers in the anthology were more taken by the ruin than we were. We were never even able to talk ourselves into the little stroll out to it. The entranceway looks like a giant stone frame, and this sometimes reminded me uncomfortably of the word-processor screen back at the office. Those who have studied the temple agree that it was never completed, but they are split as to whether it was to have been dedicated to Apollo the Sun-god or Dionysus the Wine-god. Personally, I think the temple would have been far too flattered by the sun's daily course for its location and alignment not to be intentional homage to Apollo. But I would not claim this straitlaced entranceway for the wine-god in any case.

Greek Salad

A hairclip with dangling fruits

The part of town below the Kastro is a maze of lanes riddled with shops. My daughter spent most of her holiday allowance there. She bought this whimsical barrette, for one thing. The shop where she bought it was run by a young Englishwoman who came to Naxos on holiday several years ago, fell in love with a Naxian, married him and seems virtually to have severed even mental ties to England ("I live here now."). My daughter glimpsed the husband come in and steal a kiss.

Apparently there is something peculiarly romantic in the atmosphere of Naxos. One of the island's early Western visitors, however, wrote that Naxos, despite its loveliness, is "fitter to inspire grief than joy." I suppose it could stem from the island's fecundity. The Naxians have often been remarked for their indolence, a trait invariably attributed to the supposedly effortless cultivation of their land. Kazantzakis, for that matter, was put off by the island's sweetness and languor, whether manifested in piles of ripe fruits or the taunting laugh and knees of a girl on a swing.

Speaking of Naxos and romance, my thoughts drift to Bobis, the resident Pekinese at the Anixis. Bobis will steal your heart at first glance but would sooner take off a finger than let you pet him. However, we were told that Bobis, despite his misanthropic nature, "is mad" about one young girl in the neighborhood, and we saw this for ourselves when the girl was playing with her friends in front of the hotel one day. Bobis resorted to all sorts of antics, even dragging himself on his forepaws, to keep the girl's attention. At first I thought Bobis is out of place on Naxos, where the natives otherwise accepted us into their midst without the least reservation, but now I wonder whether he is not, in his canine fashion, simply tuned in to a darkly Naxian wavelength.

A 'sfouni'

I liked Naxos right away because its heyday of tourism has yet to arrive and its shopkeepers will still entertain a foreigner's imperfect Greek rather than insist on English. In one shop the proprietress just went right on babbling in Greek to my daughter, who did not understand a word, although she was persuaded to buy several adornments anyway. While that was going on I spoke my Greek with the woman's husband and got sucked into this *sfouni*.

I was prepared to run across articles of archaic design on Naxos but I was nonetheless surprised by the *sfouni*, a ceramic device for drawing off wine from jars of an ancient type. Here is how a *sfouni* looks:

Greek Salad

I thought my find put me one up on the explorers of yesteryear until I read James Bent's extract from the 1880s in the anthology and found his description of the sfouni: "So constructed that you can fill it by suction; you then pour it out of the hole you have sucked and use the end that has been introduced into the jar for a handle." He did not give its local name, mentioning it only as "a siphon." I am embarrassed to admit that it was only after reading Bent that I realized the name sfouni is just a Naxian contraction of the ancient Greek syfoni (or syphoni).

I have a second, more elaborate sfouni that I bought from a transplanted Peloponnesian potter who preferred to transact in English. I think the handle portion was slightly botched and had to be patched over, but I bought it anyway because of its decorative color representation of a bearded Dionysus. During antiquity it was thought by many Greeks that the wine-god was born on Naxos; a 17th century explorer of the Aegean wrote that Italian mariners then still called Naxos

Aegean Islands

"Bacchus's Island." The ancient Naxians always depicted the god bearded.

A 1-liter plastic CocaCola bottle filled with wine

This was given to me as a gift by a taxi-driver, George. It's his own wine.

Old-time travelers in the Cyclades were keen to find sober muleteers, and I am always anxious to locate a solicitous taxi-driver. I spotted George and his vehicle looking squared away in the taxi line-up at the waterfront and then waited until it was his turn. I hired him to give us a tour of the interior of the island.

I could never have guessed just how suited George was to the tour I wanted. I told him of my interest in the agriculture and wine of Naxos, and my apparent seriousness of purpose resulted in an impressive outpouring of information. He explained the agricultural significance of each village or area we passed through, sometimes even giving statistics. George was somewhat formal in his delivery and, because he knew I was taking notes, he would even strike a tone of dictation from time to time, especially if the topic invited footnotes ("You should put in parentheses, that…").

George in fact was a farmer as well as a taxi-driver. On the way back to town he proposed taking us to his home in Engares, a village of western Naxos where the chief cultivations are vines, olives and citrus ("In parentheses, write 'oranges, lemons and citrons.'"). I would have liked to go, if only because the fruitfulness of Engares had contributed to Kazantzakis's squeamishness about Naxos. But my daughter by that time was carsick to the point of cursing her fate in having a Dionysus-devoted dad. George said that he would instead bring me a bottle of his wine at the Anixis. A couple of days passed and I thought he had forgotten. But on the morning of our departure he showed up at our room with this bottle.

A postcard of the village of Apiranthos

We visited Apiranthos the day George drove us. It was the finest sort of Aegean summer day – everything sparkled brilliantly and the views of Amorgos and Ikaria from the eastern side of Naxos were dream-like, as though those islands were floating out at a distant point where the Aegean and the sky melded together. We had a high vantage point too, as Naxos is the most mountainous and altitudinous of the Cyclades. In the background of this postcard you can see Mount Koronos, named for the nymph who raised Dionysus.

Apiranthos was founded several centuries ago by Cretan refugees from the Turks. The visitors of bygone centuries noted that its inhabitants were considered robbers and thugs by the other Naxians. The village headman joked with Bent that the Naxians in general have a poor reputation and that the Apiranthians are the worst of the lot. George pointed out, however, that the village is also known for its wine, figs, cheese and dry-cured ham.

George led us to a café run by the elderly Mr. Stamatoyiannis, who offered us two dry white wines and an aged, hard goat's milk cheese called "male cheese" (the village's Cretan roots could hardly be more boldly pronounced). One of the wines was excellent, while the other – which Mr. Stamatoyiannis preferred – had started to turn acidic. George, perhaps mindful of the villagers' former reputation, advised me quietly not to mention the second wine's fault.

Two Naxian wine labels

These came from Takis Probonas, the only bottler of wine on Naxos, who has a shop along the waterfront in town. His family had been distilling *kitro* since before the First World War but he expanded into wine in the 1980s when he could not help but notice that the tourists at the waterfront tables more often chose wine than *kitro*. The labels are from his two best wines, the red *Vachos* (Bacchus) and the white *Ariadni* (sic).

What better reminder of the myth of Dionysus and Ariadne? Theseus, after slaying the Minotaur, ran off with the Cretan princess Ariadne and abandoned her on Naxos. Dionysus found her and fell in love with her, but she died and the wine-god was forlorn. It seems to me an extraordinarily romantic tale for the ancient Greeks to have dreamed up, and I am not surprised that it is associated with Naxos.

Vachos and *Ariadni* are grown in Komiaki, Naxos's highest village, on the far side of Mount Koronos from Apiranthos. George took us there too, where I bought a peasant white wine made from a grape called *potamissia*. I wondered if the grape's name had any connection with the three Potamia villages in western Naxos, in the one-time deme of Biblos, whose wine was famous under the name Bibline during antiquity. The Potamia villages take their name from the rivulet that runs through them, and Dionysus was associated with the nymphs who inhabit wet places.

We went to Ano Potamia on another day so that I could investigate the grape question, but the oldest wine maker there could not tell me the origin of the name. Down a deep, lush and shaded lane beside the brook I consoled myself with the thought that I had come upon a nook where Dionysus and Ariadne must have dallied.

A 'This Summer in Naxos' guide

After looking over this guide to the island my daughter decided that we ought to try a different restaurant or *taverna* for every meal. I agreed but two exceptions occurred. One was a *taverna* that had not been advertised in the guide. It was not very attractive, and one Greek customer refused a salad because it was dressed with seed-oil instead of olive oil. We went there the first time only because it was close to where George dropped us off after our trip with him, when my daughter was still queasy and did not care where we sat down as long as we did it quickly. The *mousaka* I ate was loaded with potatoes, which gave something of a local stamp to the dish since potatoes have become the premier crop of Naxos (I learned this, of course, from George, who had discoursed longest on the subject: "Note in parentheses, that we get two crops of potatoes…"). My daughter, a potato fan, insisted on a second visit when her stomach was up to it. She was as happy with the *mousaka* as I was – although neither of us was sure about the kind of oil used.

We also ate twice at a restaurant by the sea near the Anixis, where plastic covering had to be hung on the seaward side to shield outdoor diners from the stiff breezes. The owners were a Peloponnesian and his German girlfriend, and the menu reflected their European bipolarity. While I ate Greek on our first visit and was astounded by the quality, my daughter had a Central European dish that was not all she had hoped for. As a result, she strongly opposed our second visit, which we made at my insistence on our last evening on Naxos. An acrimonious debate over the issue was followed by a silent meal. The savor of the food and wine was lost on me, and the voices of my dark mood were only drowned out whenever a truckload of potatoes bound for the ferry and the Athens market rumbled by. It seemed just as the man said of Naxos, "fitter to inspire grief than joy."

6

STATIONS

Ordinarily I let island touring take a spontaneous course. But on Kythnos I was fascinated by the rare symmetry of the bus routes and went along with the preference of my daughter, who is of a decidedly methodical cast of mind, to arrange our daily movements according to the island's bus schedules.

Kythnos has only two bus routes, and for handy reference I jotted down their schedules in my notepad:

From Merihas to Chora and Loutra: 9:30 - 11:15 - 13:15 - 16:45 - 19:00
From Loutra to Chora and Merihas: 9:00 - 10:30 - 12:15 - 16:00 - 18:00

From Merihas to Dryopida and Kanala: 7:45 - 9:40 - 11:00 - 13:15 - 17:00 - 19:00
From Kanala to Dryopida and Merihas: 8:10 - 10:00 - 11:30 - 13:45 - 17:30 - 19:30

The beauty of their layout is that the two routes are of approximately equal length and nearly reverse images of each other on a map. Both first shoot inland from the west coast terminus of Merihas at similar angles in their respective directions for half the way, and then turn outward at similar angles to continue on to their respective east coast terminuses, Loutra on the northern route and Kanala on the southern. Since Merihas is located about midway from north to south (Kythnos is longest on its north-south axis), the two routes also penetrate the island to nearly the same extent in both directions. Usually the trip from one end to the other on either route is a half hour, including halfway stops at the inland villages of Chora on the northern route and Dryopida on the southern.

*

The bus schedules I have are for Merihas because that is where we were staying. Merihas is the island's port and we never seriously considered staying anywhere else. I had called from home in the hope of making a reservation at the one full-fledged Merihas hotel, which a guidebook to Greece reported as having been closed for refurbishing but due to open again in time for the coming season. But the woman who answered the phone told me in unmistakable English that the hotel is "closed every year." It was apparent that we would have to take our chances upon arrival.

There would be plenty of daylight by which to find a room. Kythnos is the closest of the Cyclades to Piraeus and just three hours away by ferry. We arrived before noon and my daughter immediately spotted the sign of the Panorama, an attractive little three-tier layering of rooms on the hillside facing the ferry pier. She enthusiastically bounded up the several steep flights of stairs to ask about accommodations while I gratefully waited with our luggage on the street below. She was met by another teenage girl, who spoke English and represented the owners, her parents. My daughter approved the girl, the view and the room, and I signed on.

Our hosts at the Panorama were the Filippas family. Because of our daughters we spent some time with the Filipasses in their apartment above the rooms after siesta the day of our arrival. We had bowls of vanilla ice cream with liberal dollops of the family's own light and highly aromatic Kythnian honey. The Filippases told us they split their livelihood and their time between Merihas and the much larger inland village of Dryopida. They spend only the tourist season in Merihas and live in Dryopida the rest of the year; and the children, daughter and son, were attending high school in both places accordingly. Numerous other island families also participate in this contemporary form of transhumance.

*

My daughter read all the literature we had about Kythnos and decided that we ought to travel the northern bus route first. She thought the southern destinations would be more relaxing and should be saved for last.

We were out at the Merihas bus stop in time for the 9:30 trip to Loutra on the morning of our first full day on the island. Unfortunately, Kythnos had only two buses to serve its two routes and the one on the northern line had gone on the fritz on its 9:00 run from Loutra. Since I was indifferent as to whether to head north or south first, I suggested taking the southbound l0:10. But the north was already etched into my daughter's plan-of-the-day, and so, we took a taxi. Just beyond several windmills on the approach to Chora we saw the broken down bus sitting high and dry outdoors at a repair shop.

A Greek friend at home, Manolis, had encouraged us to visit Kythnos when he reminisced about a summer he spent waiting tables at a small *taverna* in Loutra. Loutra, which has only a seasonal population, is a seaside locale visited, and named, for its curative baths. Because of these thermal baths, Kythnos was known as Thermia for much of the modern era; the ancient Greeks apparently did not know them, presumably because the waters were only revealed by a later eruption of the now extinct volcano that is the blunt hill seen behind Loutra. My daughter wanted to get Loutra out of the way and off her tour list since neither of us was ailing from anything that the baths might remedy.

The taxi driver, as if by long habit, automatically dropped us off right in front of the little spa. We followed the curve of the bay on foot as far as a homey *taverna* standing along the way out to an abandoned ore-tip (iron ore used to be mined on Kythnos). An elderly woman and her daughter-in-law were sitting in the shade of an arbor over the second-floor veranda and cutting up potatoes and other vegetables that they then tossed into airtight plastic-ware to be stored in the refrigerator until the evening, the only time the *taverna* was open for business. The husband of the older woman came up the stairs a few minutes later carrying a watermelon from the garden, and he cut slices for us. We thought it the sweetest watermelon we had ever tasted. I did not mention my friend Manolis because it was only when we were back by the baths that I recalled his description of the *taverna*'s location and realized that it tallied with where we had been.

*

With the bus still in the repair shop, the 12:15 from Loutra was also cancelled. But we had no trouble catching a ride back to Chora since taxis were bringing new ferry arrivals from Merihas to the spa about that time.

We thought we might be completely wasting our time in Chora because of a travel book that all but called the village ugly. The writer must have confused his notes with some other place – or else we were observing the wrong features.

Admittedly our eyes oftentimes were trained downward as we strolled through the village. We were looking at the carefree white designs of flowers and

Greek Salad

fish that brighten the pavement in Chora's lanes. On account of our inattentiveness to what was ahead of us we even lost our way once and covered the same ground twice. I had to ask for directions out of the village from a man who was standing just inside the open doorway of his home. He turned out to be an Athenian who was married to a woman originally from Kythnos. The couple had a house and spent their summers on the island.

I also asked the man about local wine since Chora is the settlement closest to Kythnos's main agricultural area, and he took us to a household that makes its own. The wine had a slightly resinous flavor just as a result of having been stored in a barrel that had been rubbed with resin on the inside. The explorer James Bent reported in the late 19th century that Kythnos was the only island of the Cyclades where he found *retsina*. This habit possibly originated with the repopulation of the island several centuries ago, when Albanians from the eastern mainland of Greece were enticed to Kythnos. Even though all other traces of the Albanians have been lost, they were familiar with resination and apparently left that behind as their legacy.

My Athenian interlocutor, sniffing beneath the resin, said approvingly but tentatively that the wine smelled like *alimia*, and added that when he was a child during the Second World War his family occasionally had to eat *alimia*. Then he sniffed again and affirmed the smell as that of *alimia*. I wish I could have been able to nod knowingly in agreement, but actually I did not have any idea whether he might be right. I inferred that *alimia* is a plant, and later I learned that it is in fact a coastal bush whose Latin name is *atriplex halimus,* or sea orach in English. But even that knowledge would have been of no use to me in Chora because of my lack of nose-on experience. Sometimes the sensory world of Greece is off limits to me even if not quite beyond my appreciation.

*

The next day was devoted to the southern bus route. We went down to the Merihas stop to catch the 9:40 to Dryopida. The northern bus was back in commission and standing next to ours to await passengers for its 9:30 run to Loutra.

Dryopida is nestled down amidst a patch of rolling hills to escape notice by the pirates who plagued the Cyclades in the Middle Ages. Few tourists spy its charm today. Our own curiosity was whetted primarily by the Filipasses, and the more so for me when their daughter, predictably enough even in the Cyclades for a sixteen-year-old, confirmed the least of my fears engendered by travel books, that "nothing happens" in Dryopida.

Mrs. Filippas had mentioned a family of potters in Dryopida and we managed to find their workshop. An elderly man and woman were on the premises. The man said he was the third generation of his family doing this work, and that both his son and grandson were following in his footsteps. He whipped up a vase on his wheel while we talked. We would have bought a finished piece for a souvenir, but the ones we liked were quite bulky and Kythnian clay seemed exceedingly heavy. We had already saddled ourselves with a one-kilogram plastic jar of honey that we bought from a woman in the village.

The potters were also making cheese. Kythnian cheese has been famous since antiquity, when it was mentioned by Aristotle, Pliny and, of course, Epicurus. This cheese is not a *feta*, but rather a fresh cheese that could become *feta* were the butter taken off. The quality and character of the cheese are attributed to a particular wild plant that grows on Kythnos and is preferred by the sheep and goats. We were already familiar with the cheese from the *taverna*s in Merihas, where it appears in fried cheese-balls, called *sfoungato*, the local specialty. But at the pottery we tasted it in its natural state. The cheese is made in earthenware forms, which perhaps explains a potter's particular interest in it. I bought a bit to accompany the honey, and besides, on a volume basis, Kythnian cheese is featherweight compared to Kythnian clay.

*

We took the 14:00 bus (the 13:45 from Kanala) back to Merihas because Dryopida had no place where we could get a meal. We could have continued on from Dryopida to Kanala on the 13:15 from Merihas, but no bus would be returning from Kanala until 17:30 and we had not wanted to spend that part of the day at the beach. The Filippas girl had told us that Kanala had the best beach accessible to us, as visitors without our own vehicle or boat, and we were doing all of our swimming in the afternoon when the intensity of the sun was abating. After lunch and siesta in Merihas we were back on the road with the 17:00 bus to Kanala. We had our bathing suits on underneath our clothing.

The bus line to Kanala ends by the little monastery of Panayia of Kanala that sits at the head of a short cape. The church on the monastery grounds contains the icon of the Virgin Mary (Panayia) that local fishermen found at the bottom of the bay. Our visit was punctuated by the repeated shrewish hollering of a woman who wanted her two boys to get down off the church's roof. Kanala seemed to be populated entirely by Athenian families who were renting summer homes across from the monastery.

A bright green patch of refreshing pines spread from the monastery down to the sea. An old Kythnian oral tradition has it that the island at one time had stands of trees, but the reference obviously must be to a time that was literally ages ago, before inhabitants and pirates cut them down for their needs. Except for some scattered almonds, figs and olives, Kythnos's only trees today are the ones at Kanala. Travel books had almost steered us away from Kythnos by dwelling on the island's bareness.

When we returned from the beach the *taverna* adjoining the monastery was preparing for the evening trade and had lamb, kid and *kokoretsi* (seasoned lamb offal wrapped in intestines) turning on spits. It was appetizing, but we felt clammy in our bathing suits and decided to catch the last bus, the 19:30, back to Merihas instead of hanging around in Kanala. We discovered on the road back that Kythnos's brown and lumpy land is bewitching as the sun goes down.

*

We did not at all mind returning to Merihas for dinner. Our favorite *taverna* was there, Yialos (Seashore). The chef prepared fish expertly in the traditional Cycladic way for each kind. Even my daughter was lured away from her landlubber Greek favorites once. Most permanent residents of Merihas are fisher folk, and the fish offered at Yialos varied daily according to the previous night's catch. The island's waters are highly esteemed Aegean fishing grounds. Fish obviously find nothing unattractive about Kythnos's looks from their perspective.

I would have liked to stay on Kythnos several days more with nothing much to do other than to swim and enjoy fish at Merihas. But in the wee hours of the next morning my daughter awoke twice screaming after apparently being bitten by something. We found the culprit after the second time, a kind of prehistoric millipede about three-inches long and three-sixteenths of an inch wide. I shook the insect off the sheet and onto the floor, where I stomped it for my daughter's peace of mind, but it did not die easily and did not squash at all. I left the ribbon-like carcass on the floor to show to the Filippases, but they had never seen its likes before. Kythnos's earliest known name was Ofiousa, which referred to the extraordinary population of snakes it apparently had when it was still forested, and the island is known to harbor strange critters even now.

Mrs. Filippas gave my daughter some ointment for her wounds. "Boy," reflected the victim in the wake of her ordeal, "Kythnos has special cheese, weird vegetation and its own bug." It is not usually easy to know when to call it quits on an island visit, but I realized then that we had done the circuit on Kythnos.

7

AN ILL WIND

Disembarkation from an Aegean ferry is a predictable experience. The passengers going ashore gather aft in the cavity of the ferry and anxiously await mooring and the lowering of the stern ramp. With the initial slackening of the ropes restraining the ramp, the assembly closes ranks as involuntarily as a sphincter. The thumping and scraping sounds of the steel ramp touching down on the concrete wharf send a new shiver of tension through the swarm and all debarkees grab their baggage, grit their teeth and prepare to jostle. As soon as the ramp is securely positioned and the engines are cut, a ship's officer gives the Go signal and the body touristic trundles forward over the ramp and onto the new lounging grounds. Since the embarkees must also be brought aboard expeditiously, their vanguard inevitably collides with the rear guard of the debarkees. Only a few such experiences are needed to develop the knack of desensitizing oneself to all of it, but in any case the immediate surroundings and the logistics of the event generally do not permit keeping one disembarkation distinct from another in one's memory.

Serifos, however, was a different experience when my daughter and I arrived. It was close to noon on a Sunday in July. As soon as the ramp began to be lowered, a howling mélange of sounds which could have played second fiddle to Homeric sirens seeped into the ferry's cavern. When the ramp was one-third down, whistling winds and human voices could be made out, with the voices sounding almost like a chant, as if striking dockworkers were protesting or a political figure was being welcomed. By the time the ramp was halfway down we could see that forceful winds of the *meltemi* were whipping the sea up against the wharf and that several men were singing and dancing to the music of a violin and lute. My daughter wondered if the men's performance might be a routine summertime welcome for arriving ferries, like the hula dancers who used to meet the ocean liners arriving in Hawaii. But these patently ordinary locals were so ecstatic and doing such a capital job of keeping time to the music and in step with each other, that they had to be in the hands of the Muses – and not quite sober from Saturday night. I knew it for sure when a woman further down the wharf remarked, "They're dancing again." I took an immediate shine to Serifos.

We were at Livadi, the chief tourist haven of the island. Livadi owes its touristic role in part to its being a port, but more so to its good long beachfront. A line of hotels, *taverna*s, cafés and suntan lotion shops extends halfway along the beach. But Livadi lies open to the *meltemi* and is attacked by it head on from the north. The *meltemi* kicks up sand on the beach and dirt on the unpaved roadway that parallels the beach. Owners of beachfront buildings hose down their portion of road so as to lend the dirt some weight and wind-resistance, which exacerbates the summer water shortage but adds to Livadi's down-home charm.

I should have made a hotel reservation since it was the last week of July, when the tourist season begins to peak. I did not do it because I had been on the verge of cutting Serifos from our itinerary. A German family we met on Kythnos told us that they had already spent a week on Serifos, in Livadi, and that the nightly noise from the bars there was inescapable. My daughter persuaded me to stick to our original schedule and give Serifos at least a one-night trial, but I wanted to size up the touristic terrain on the spot before settling on accommodations.

From on deck as the ferry approached Livadi I had noticed a several-story white hotel set back from the beach about midway down the line of mostly two-story buildings. Leaving my daughter with our luggage at the head of the dirt roadway, I went to have a closer look and found the hotel situated at an encouraging distance from entertainment that might blare for attention until a late hour. It was sheltered further by a muffle of trees. I thought we stood a good chance of being able to sleep, and we were in luck because a room had just been vacated (the parades of debarking and embarking Aegean ferry passengers represent a complex swapping of beds and deck seats).

The hotel was one of that Aegean class for which a substantial initial investment was made some years earlier, but whose original qualities have never been tampered with thereafter, notwithstanding the recurrent yearly round of 'hot beds' played by the ferry passengers. A pre-summer whitewash to maintain outward appearances is the main upkeep expense. The somewhat tatty condition of our hotel added to the feeling I already had, just from walking down Livadi's shady main drag, of being on the set of a 1940s movie starring Humphrey Bogart as a deadbeat stranded in the tropics. Even the hotel's operator was perfectly suited to his part, a seedy old guy with a thin but shapeless mustache, slicked-back hair that was unruly at the fringes and sagging pants that had to be hiked up every couple of minutes if he happened to be moving about. And the more the *meltemi* rustled the reeds outside, the more I thought of the old movies. I half expected a sultry young Greek Lauren Bacall to emerge from a hallway into the lobby. But all that ever actually appeared was a miscast pair of frumpy Polish room maids.

Only a summertime visitor without a hotel reservation would have been surveying Livadi intently as the ferry approached. It is Chora, the upland settlement seen behind Livadi, which is bound to catch and hold anyone else's eye. Chora makes a fairy tale climb in three stages up a jagged little peak set in the middle of a stiff bright meringue of higher ones. The magic of the picture must be there even without Chora, however. Serifos's appearance was explained anciently by the myth of Perseus, according to which he turned his adversaries into stone sculptures by circumnavigating the island and displaying before their eyes the severed head of Medusa, the snaky haired gorgon.

Rather than take a siesta that might leave us too well rested to defy a din and be able to sleep at night, we took a bus up to Chora after lunch. We did not have a real choice of destinations because the only pavement on Serifos went from Livadi to Chora and then to the hamlet of Kentarhos, and the bus connection operated only along the first leg. I also wanted to see Chora right away to check on the availability of rooms in the event that Livadi did not work out, since the German couple said that Chora was absolutely peaceful, and that they had seen a few signs there advertising rooms. But in looking out at Serifos from the ferry the overall logistical advantage was with Livadi. Not to mention that it was doubtful what I might face in carting our train of luggage up and down through Chora. As it happened, the first thing we saw in Chora as we stepped off the bus was two men hauling a new refrigerator up an adjacent incline. The larger man was walking bent over with the refrigerator bound to his back with a rope while the smaller one was giving token support from the rear by holding the bottom of the refrigerator. I saw an analogy to me and my daughter.

The only sightseeing obligation in Chora is to visit the tiny chapel atop the peak and enjoy the view down to Livadi. Most of our time was spent fifty meters be-

Aegean Islands

low on the little *plateia*, which would be the perfect image of an Aegean village square – white, simple, angular – were it not for the neo-classical town hall raised in a dark fit of neo-Hellenic megalomania early in the 20th century. The square was dead quiet except for the gusting of winds finding their way into or out of the space, but at one of its corners the entrance to a Lilliputian cook-shop named Piatsa was wide open. We spent the next hour or more seated inside the Piatsa as cozy as anyone could have felt in Robert Louis Stevenson's Admiral Benbow Inn on a blustery winter day.

I lost all sense of altitude in the Piatsa and fancied myself along a waterfront during a gale. Although the interior did not have a nautical motif, the high ceiling, bare rafters and enclosed half-attic made me think of an old-time ship chandlery. Three tables, each two-feet square in surface, were in the front half of the room, with a refrigerated display case separating them from the kitchen cubicle in the back half. The kitchen could have been a ship's galley from the days of sail, and in my Treasure Island state of mind I imagined Long John Silver wheeling around in it ever so handily on his crutch to fix a hash.

The Piatsa was a *mezethopoleion*, a kind of *taverna* dedicated to serving warm *mezethes* with wine or *ouzo*. The menu of about a dozen offerings was in proportion to the kitchen. Assorted beverages were stocked inside the display case, and all along its top stood amateurishly labeled bottles of a blond wine. The label bore the obscure name *Vlataki* and a map of Serifos with a conspiratorial X drawn freehand at a spot near Chora. I ordered a half-bottle of the wine along with a plate of wild-fennel fritters to keep me on an even keel.

The place was being operated by the Maroulis family – husband, wife and daughter, respectively the provisioner, the cook and the server. They had spent twelve years in New Jersey and they admitted that re-adjustment to life on Serifos had been difficult. The cost of living was no compensation, either. Mrs. Maroulis said that goods in Chora can cost up to four times as much as they would in Athens because of transportation costs, including Athens to Piraeus, Piraeus to Serifos, and Livadi up to Chora (my thoughts flew to refrigerators). Their only income now was from Piatsa, and most of their endeavors were in support of their business. All the herbs and vegetables used in the kitchen came from the family's own fields and gardens, and *Vlataki* was grown in their vineyard, which had that name and was located at the spot marked by the X on the label map. I thought all this a quiet contentment after a dozen years in Jersey.

After leaving the Piatsa we returned to the bus stop. We found a bus but no driver or other sign of impending activity. A building with the sign 'Stavros' was nearby and we went over to it in the hope of gaining some information about the bus's departure time.

Aegean Islands

We were greeted immediately at the doorway by Stavros himself, a short and portly man in his sixties, who advised us that we would have to wait another half hour for the bus. He invited us in to sit and elude the *meltemi* in the meantime.

It was not evident just what kind of catering establishment Stavros was running. The room was long and narrow and had several largish plate glass windows that offered a smudgy panorama down to the sea from one side of Chora. Although some kitchen fixtures and cooking equipment were in the far end of the room I did not inquire about them lest Stavros urge some unwanted dish on us. But I helped myself to a club soda from the cold-drink storage unit near the entrance and paid before taking a seat. Stavros seated himself against the wall directly across from us and began making conversation.

Stavros had spent his career at sea as a cook on ocean liners. During 1964-66 he had done a stint on the Greek Lines' *Olympia*, the very ship on which, in 1963, I made my first trip to Greece. We even remembered the same captain. Stavros had also done some world traveling under his own steam in the years since his retirement, though by way of Olympic Airways. He pointed to a Greek travel poster on the wall behind him. The poster showed a black-and-white photograph of a man seated against a white Aegean storefront. He was wearing a wide-brimmed hat and his forehead was resting on his arms, which were

Greek Salad

folded across the back of another chair in front of him; his face could not be seen. Stavros said the man was his father and that the picture had been taken in Chora fifty years earlier. The poster was still current, though, and Stavros reported seeing it himself in an Olympic Airways lounge in Honolulu.

A young Greek couple came in to buy bottled water out of the cooler and asked Stavros about ferries from Serifos to Paros. They were fed up with the *meltemi* and thought they would escape it on Paros. Stavros did not try to argue that the *meltemi* would be just as ruinous of a holiday on Paros, but he did try to dissuade the couple by assuring them that the wind would die down in a day or two, and by warning them of the horde of tourists they would face on Paros. "We know all about Paros," the woman shot back, leaving it to her tone to convey the unspoken words, "you old fool."

When we awoke the next morning in our hotel room (after a night of sleep undisturbed by Livadi revelry), the *meltemi* was still on. At breakfast downstairs two middle-aged Greek couples seated at separate tables were discussing the inconvenience of the wind with the hotel owner, who was seated at a third table. The one couple had only arrived the day before and were worried about driving their rental car over mountain byways subject to strong blasts of air. The other couple had been on Serifos long enough to remember when the *meltemi* was not blowing and roundly criticized the local authorities, the Greek government and the European Union for letting Livadi's beachside thoroughfare remain a dust bin. The hotelkeeper's best advice was that they all go bathing at Ganema, which he said was protected from the *meltemi*.

My daughter and I had no desire for a morning swim but she thought we might hike out to Ganema just to see more of the island. I agreed after looking at my map and gauging Ganema to be about four miles away. We had the wind at our backs and made the first couple of miles comfortably enough, pausing now and then to admire the scenes wrought by Medusa's head. But soon afterward the roadway led upward between two closely situated mountainous formations where the *meltemi* was working a wind tunnel. The force pushing us forward became more powerful as we ascended. The road disappeared at a turn dead ahead, and the open sky at the turn suggested a cliff or some other rocky drop. With my daughter's ninety pounds of flesh about to set sail in that direction, we scratched Ganema and, with effort, backtracked.

The bus for Chora happened to be standing at the ready when we got back to Livadi. On the spur of the moment we hopped aboard to go and have lunch at Piatsa. We had an appetite and ordered fully half of the menu, so that even the ashtray had to be removed from our table in order to accommodate all the dishes. We listened to the wind and talked to the Maroulises again, and left with a souvenir bottle of *Vlataki* a couple of hours later.

Walking down from the *plateia* into the lower section of Chora we found a very old woman and a much younger one sitting in front of a little sundries shop. The young woman was from Athens and said she and her husband had bought the house right across the lane. No sooner had she finished telling us this than a woman came out of the house next to hers and began scolding her about the condition of her patch of stone patio. The Athenian told her to mind her own business and the neighbor stomped back into her house. I went over to the patio to take a look at what the fuss was about and saw dried paint drippings in one small corner of the space. The woman took a drag on her cigarette and complained that most of the locals resent outsiders, especially Athenians, who come and buy houses. She said the price of everything on the island rises to meet the more demanding Athenian standard of comfort.

The next day had to be our last on Serifos in order to return to Athens and meet some friends. We were catching a late afternoon ferry. There was no time for a relaxed taxi trip to Kentarhos at the far end of the island's freeway. Instead we headed on foot for Psili Ammos beach to have a look at the 'fine sand' for which it is named and praised. But since Psili Ammos was in the opposite direction from Ganema we had to walk into the *meltemi* most of the time. This gave us a preview of the beachside sandblasts we would be in for. We turned back three-quarters of an hour later after deciding that we must surely have seen equally fine sand somewhere on Atlantic shores back home.

The *meltemi* was more robust than ever that afternoon when we went out to the wharf to catch the ferry. Among the embarkees was the couple from our hotel who had rented the car. Apparently they had given up on the prospect of the *meltemi* ever abating. The sea sprayed us regularly as we waited on the wharf; and the ferry was nearly an hour late because the weather had slowed its progress north from Milos and Sifnos. When it finally arrived and the debarkees started passing by, a young Greek waiting to board with his motorcycle smirked and quipped to his hip companions, "They don't know what they're in for."

I was pushing my handbag forward in the queue with my foot and it happened to strike the bottle of *Vlataki* stored inside. I thought of the map on its label and reflected that we were leaving Serifos without having been to any part of it that we could not see from the deck of the ferry the day we arrived. I could have cursed the *meltemi* had it not been for all the extras it had thrown our way.

8

POT LUCK

The summer of our visit to the western Cyclades was otherwise marked by my daughter's first committed foray into the kitchen. Without any early warning signs she suddenly began paging through all the cookbooks at home, including several Greek ones, and launched a successful coup to take over the stove. As an outgrowth of her new interest she was keen to have "authentic" food on our trip, by which she had in mind local dishes that the natives make for themselves when the tourists are not around. Culinary curiosity indeed was the keynote of our days on Milos and Sifnos.

The bogus and the bona fide were not easy to sort out on Milos. Disillusionment descended on us almost every time we thought we had authenticity in the bag. We were even beset by nomenclature traps. There was, for instance, the English-language menu sign announcing "egg plants cookenshop meat," which we imagined to be a rare Milean specialty, but which turned out to be just a disaggregated English rendering of *mousaka*.

Our basic error on Milos may have been a tactical one. We had reserved a room in Adamas, the main port, whose Milean credentials are weak. Adamas was founded by Cretan refugees from Ottoman rule early in the 20th century. But genuineness even of a Cretan kind eluded us. The first time we entered an Adamas *taverna* we walked over to the open kitchen to inquire about the day's specials, as is customary throughout Greece, and were sullenly ordered to take a seat outside and await a server who, we were instructed in no uncertain terms, would come and tell us what we needed to know. We moved on rather than take a seat, but affectation, not to mention crabbiness and hostility, was the order of the day in other Adamas eateries as well. Any residual ancestral Cretan pride seemed to have degenerated, whether or not under the pressure of tourism, into disdain.

In the face of our mealtime frustration my daughter sought between-meals compensation in dough. Her culinary efforts at home had been concentrated primarily on baking, and pastry became a daily salve for our psyches on Milos. She really became preoccupied with cookies, however. Adamas's one saving grace, from her perspective, was its sole bakery, which we discovered on our first afternoon. The bakery was located near the Church of Ayia Triada (Holy Trinity) that we had gone to see on the hill dominating Adamas. A priest who was in the church pointed out 13th and 14th century icons brought by the Cretan founders, but my daughter was far more taken by the cookies from various eras of Aegean history that were arrayed in the bakery. Over the next four days we tried all the cookies, at the rate of three to six new kinds daily, in proportion to the degree of our frustration on Milos.

Greek Salad

We were reluctant to give up on Milos gastronomically despite the string of rebuffs we suffered at the hands of Adamas caterers. The island can excite the mind to gustatory anticipation just by its impressive topographical and geological diversity, which promises a microcosm of Cycladic flavors. And the broad Kambos area stretching back from the low ground behind the airport and fading away on the gentle slopes in the distance is as promising an expanse of cultivable land as is to be found in the Cyclades.

Thinking that some solid agricultural information might come in handy in sniffing out truly local dishes, I contacted the island's farm cooperative association. Their chief agronomist had his office just off the main street in the hill village of Pera Triovasalos. He informed us that Milos produces various fruits and vegetables, wines, olive oil and ewe's and goat's milk cheeses, and all for local consumption, without reference to the tastes of the Greek or international markets. He gave us an especially detailed rundown on cheeses, but that was as close as he came to gastronomy as such. The leap from cottage to kitchen was too great for him and what happens to Milean products after they leave the field or the processing facilities was all but a mystery to him. He demurred even on dispensing any *taverna* tips.

Our big break came late on our third afternoon when we least expected it. We had just come back to Adamas after a long walk along the road that hugs the vast bay of Milos. The walk was marred by another hapless encounter with natives. We had come to a utilitarian building and landscaped grounds that looked like they might possibly comprise a minor agricultural research site. An elderly couple was stopped there with their car, which had local license plates, and I asked about the building, only to have the man growl back, "What do you want to know for?" Obviously we would have to lick our wounds at the bakery again, but this time we found our way there by a different route and on the way met Katerina Kalotsi and Yeoryios Nouardos, a couple more than happy to share whatever they knew about Milos.

Katerina and Yeoryios were not from Adamas. They were not even Mileans. They were from Thessaloniki and only spent their summers on Milos, where they operated a shop selling Katerina's artwork. She worked mainly in ceramics and turned out decorative pieces that drew heavily on ancient mythology in highly original ways. A favorite subject for her work was Aphrodite, the goddess who sprang up from the foam of the sea. Aphrodite is connected with Milos because of the statue Venus de Milo (actually Aphrodite of Milos). We had already been to the archaeological museum in the island capital of Plaka and seen the replica that the French sent to the Mileans to replace the real thing, which stands in the Louvre. My daughter, in her fervor for genuine articles, had been peeved about the French over Venus and saw

Greek Salad

Katerina's pieces most favorably – that is, on a par with the cookies in authenticity.

We spent some time with Katerina and Yeoryios both that afternoon and the next. Yeoryios poured me some of his own wine from Macedonia the second time. He had nothing against local farm products, though. Far from it, he took a dim view of the uniformity he saw creeping into Greek cuisine as a consequence of industrialization and tourism, and had rather a gourmand's interest in typical Milean foods. Patting his developing midriff to assure us that he knew what he was talking about, Yeoryios handed me the card of O Hamos *taverna* in Pera Triovasalos.

We might have passed by O Hamos the day we went to the agronomist's office. Belying its name, which translates roughly as 'Ruckus,' the *taverna* was small, unobtrusive and easy to miss. In any case, O Hamos was specialized strictly in devil-may-care, high-cholesterol *mezethes* that obviously would appeal to Yeoryios – each was like a small meal. The evening of our visit the menu featured kid livers, kid baked with lemon sauce in individual ceramic casseroles, and pork baked in similar casseroles with wine, wild herbs, carrots and two of the Milean cheeses the agronomist had told us about. Virtually all of our dinner came from the garden, vineyard and animals of our hosts, the Psathas family, and Mrs. Psathas was generous enough to share the recipe for the baked pork casserole. We left Milos the next day with a sense of culinary discovery that not even the cookies of Adamas would have allowed.

*

It was well after dark when we arrived from Adamas to the port of Kamares on Sifnos. We did not reach our lodgings at the tiny Hotel Sifnos in the inland capital of Apollonia for another half hour. The last ten minutes were an upward pull on foot with our luggage since the hotel was far up the village's narrow main lane from where the taxi had to leave us off. Famished by that time, we were quite willing to settle for the hotel's fare at a table under the trees of the adjacent small square. If only one had always to 'settle' for a meal like the one we got that evening: carefully spiced Sifnian fried chickpea balls and wonderfully herbed, expertly grilled, mouthwatering swordfish kebabs.

I took the opportunity of the meal to reiterate to my daughter that Sifnos has a solid reputation for its cooks. There was even a time in the 19th century when practically all the professional cooks of Constantinople (today's Istanbul) were Sifnians. And Greece's best known chef of the 20th century, Nicholas Tselementes, who at one time was called in to direct the kitchens of the Hotel St. Moritz in New York, was a native of Sifnos. My daughter was already familiar with his book on Greek cookery and was planning to make his Sifnian honey-and-cheese pie.

Greek Salad

Our host at the Hotel Sifnos was Apostolos Diaremis, bearded and constantly outfitted in black jeans and cowboy belt. He must have been keeping an eye open for us the evening of our arrival because he called out my name by way of inquiry as soon as he spotted us coming up the lane. Mr. Diaremis, who always seemed two steps ahead in touristic strategy, doubtlessly had been worried he might have a vacant room on his hands that night. When I phoned him from Athens to confirm our reservation he said he had yet to receive my bank draft for the deposit he had requested, although I sent it two months previously. He had still not seen the draft when we arrived.

At breakfast on the veranda the next morning, Mr. Diaremis came over to our table elatedly and announced that the draft had been found. His mother had received the envelope and misfiled it under my first name instead of my last. He continued and said that he had read the letter I sent with the draft, in which I told him we would be grateful for any guidance he could provide about Sifnian foods. He took a seat with us and offered to tell us anything we wanted to know. It was one of the very few times we saw Mr. Diaremis when he was neither darting purposefully about the premises nor stroking his beard in deliberation. It was apparent that he was not a little fond of the subject of interest to us. In fact we would have a couple more chats with him about Sifnian food and each time he concluded with an expression of frustration about the bulge at his ornamented Western belt buckle.

Aegean Islands

My daughter started off by asking Mr. Diaremis about the ingredients for *biskotakia*, the lightly almond-flavored Sifnian cookies that came with the Hotel Sifnos breakfast, and which she declared superior to any of the Milean cookies we had tried. As we would find almost invariably when moved to gastronomic admiration on Sifnos, the ingredients were plain, it was the skill of the practitioner that was telling.

The most typical dish of Sifnos is merely baked chickpeas, *revithia fournou*, a fixture of Sunday dinners that bakes in a slow oven all night Saturday. Mr. Diaremis regretted that we would not be staying through Sunday, because the baked chickpeas are on the hotel menu that day. Real beans were available everywhere the rest of the week, but we had been warned away from them by a Greek friend at home who told us that the soil of Sifnos has an unusually high content of nitrogen, which saturates ordinary beans and can have a powerful "dehydrating" effect on unaccustomed digestive systems. (When he and his wife visited Sifnos they had an immobilizing encounter with *mavromatika* beans in particular. "We stayed in the room dehydrated for two days.") Consequently we never dared to venture beyond fried chickpea balls in the legume category while on Sifnos. But we liked those so well that we ordered them with all of our meals and upon returning home were disappointed to find that Chef Tselementes had not included a recipe for them in his book.

Greek Salad

We returned to Kamares the next day to explore the pottery shops that had also been mentioned to us by our informant on nitrogen. Pottery is a very old Sifnian specialty and likely was a factor contributing to culinary expertise. Even the local word for pottery, *tsikalaria*, refers to a piece of specialized cookware, the *tsikali revithiou*, the pot for the baked chickpeas. (Tselementes gave no recipe for the baked chickpeas, either. Presumably that was because he thought nobody but a Sifnian was likely to have either the patience or the pot to prepare the dish in the way needed to lift chickpeas above their lowly gastronomic station.) I was not in the market for a *tsikali*, but I almost bought a *kotopouliera*, a sort of ceramic tandoor for baking a chicken, from a grandmotherly woman in one of the pottery shops. I may have been overcome by the delightful smells wafting out of the kitchen in the rear of the shop. But my daughter persuaded me that the *kotopouliera* was too plump and fragile for us to carry home. We settled on a more symbolic allusion to Sifnian epicurean concerns, a delicate ceramic pomegranate.

As long as I was on Sifnos again I wanted to revisit the authenticity I had experienced in the village of Artemona eleven years earlier when I had been sent from the island of Paros just to eat roast lamb and drink local *retsina* at O Manganas *taverna*. The major villages of Sifnos fringe an amphitheater of intensively cultivated terraces and Artemona is only a twenty-minute walk from Apollonia.

Aegean Islands

I recognized the main square of Artemona, but that was my only clue to the whereabouts of O Manganas. The former grill-room had expanded during the intervening years and become the most touted restaurant in the western Cyclades, To Liotrivi (The Olive Mill). The menu had grown exponentially to keep pace with fame, and my suspicion was that high-season diners were now on their own in picking out authenticity. We certainly were not going to order *mastello*, which is lamb baked with wine on a bed of vine cuttings, all of which is placed inside an earthenware pot of that name. Mr. Diaremis had advised us that the only true season for the dish is Eastertide, because of the qualities of the lamb meat and the condition of the vine cuttings at that time, and that entrepreneurs who put it on the menu for summer tourists do not even adhere to the orthodox baking procedure, another overnight affair.

Our stay on Sifnos lasted a day longer than planned, but we could not remain at the Hotel Sifnos since according to Mr. Diaremis's up-to-the-hour accounting it was already fully and foolproof-ly booked. We managed to find another room situated along the road above Apollonia and conveniently accessible to the village's main lane. Our second room was also close to the neighboring village of Exambela, which happens to be the birthplace of Nicholas Tselementes.

Mr. Diaremis said that the Tselementes family, although no longer resident on the island, still have their ancestral house in Exambela, and a dated Greek-language guide to Sifnos (published while the arch-chef was still living) mentioned that the house is situated behind Ayios Yeoryios church. We took a stroll through the village our last afternoon and readily found the church, but we were not sure which house might be that of the Tselementes family, and not a soul was in sight to ask. I half expected that the Sifnians would have put up a bronze bust of a be-tocqued Chef Nick, or perhaps a brass plaque on the house, or in some other way have memorialized their master crafts-man in his native village, as they have proudly done for their poets and pedagogues. But they had not. "Well," remarked my daughter, the baker's apprentice, "he was only a cook."

9

BRAVING THE ELEMENTS

Santorini can devastate the newcomer. One American woman told me that she knew nothing about the island, not even about its sunken volcano, when she casually went along with her husband's suggestion that they visit. They arrived by air from Athens at night, and consequently the next morning she still had no inkling of the scene of Santorini with its great half-moon bay and satellite islets. Then, while out exploring the countryside with her husband, she suddenly happened upon a panoramic view of the curve of crater cliffs that fall several hundred feet into the bay. She was at once beside herself and tears streamed down her face.

In my own case I arrived by ferry and had time to assimilate the island's aspect as we entered the bay, but I was overcome nonetheless. The bay actually is a caldera formed by a horrific eruption about 1600 B.C. and is too deep to allow anchoring. Eerie preternatural forces worked on me while the ferry was moored offshore and boats came out to take us ashore. The dead calm of the evening sea around the island caused me to notice a peculiar rhythm, a just slightly perceptible decomposure of the water within the enclosure of the bay, as though the bay were a jar of water shaken a few moments ago in geological time. And although it was dusk the variously shaded cliffs were enveloped

Greek Salad

by a darkness that was not entirely owing to the hour – something malevolent about Santorini's very nature made it forbidding even to look at the cliffs. The air was cool and fresh yet at the same time vaguely stifling, as if the volcano below the islet in the middle of the bay was gently exhaling a substance inimical to Earth's creatures. The experience altogether gave me a very visceral sense of nature's havoc wreaked and I was feeling emotionally drained by the time we reached the landing.

And then there was my daughter, who on her first visit lost it completely when she suffered a middle-of-the-night upheaval after overindulging on Santorini's double-strength dwarf tomatoes.

*

Dehydration is natural to Santorini and not everyone has the stomach for it. The Ottomans, for instance, gave Santorini an agglutinative Turkish sobriquet signifying 'place to abandon for good.' The old name will seem ironic to anyone who has been caught in a traffic jam in the cliff-side capital of Fira at the height of the summer, when transients seem never to leave. But whereas the Turks were not up to the austere regimen imposed by the island's lack of water, today's seasonal subjugators essentially are mortifiers of the flesh.

Aegean Islands

Dehydration nowadays is practiced primarily on Santorini's beaches. These beaches vary in geological origin and come in three colors: white, red and black. Opinions differ as to the efficacy of the several beaches in achieving doneness. Having resolutely avoided sidling for space on the beaches, I have no firsthand opinion except to observe that the parched sunbather of summer is at best only an unfinished fore-runner of Santorini's dried-pork *pasto* meat of winter.

The true Santorinian does have in common with the summer crowd a predilection for dessication. It used to be, before the arrival of the jet set on the beaches, that the island plain was the main arena for dehydration, where peasants spread crops like fava peas and grapes in the sun to dry after harvesting. Dried fava provides mealy substance for a number of local dishes. Grapes subjected to sunbathing go to make sweet wines, such as the paradoxically unctuous *visanto*, from which all superfluous moisture has been removed. Like the beaches, sweet wines come in white, red or black and have their adherents respectively.

It was wine rather than beaches that won Santorini its first constant foreign sympathizers, the Russians. In the 19th century the Russians had an unquenchable thirst for the island's bacchic answer to potable water. In contrast the French in those days took a rather Turkish view of Santorini and kept their distance. They claimed to identify in the taste of Santorinian wines the island's calamitous geological past and lacked the fortitude of the earthy Russians to bear it.

*

Everybody should expect to endure overexposure on Santorini. Daytime arrivals by ferry routinely suffer to cool their heels on the wharf at Athinios while waiting for a ride up to the plain and Fira. And the risk is almost as great on the plain itself. The plain, which was once a skirt of the volcano and slopes eastward from the rim of the caldera, is practically without trees or shade, and the chances are that public transportation, being inadequate for the summer swarms, will sooner or later leave one hanging out to dry.

My daughter and I spent close to an hour seated on a low stone wall at an intersection near the village of Kamari on the eastern, seaward side of the island, hoping for either a bus or a taxi with room available to take us back to Fira. A middle-aged peasant woman who improbably could manage conversation in English joined us on the wall, and she was followed by a sullen youth from Albania who was earning his fava as a day laborer. The woman threw in the towel after twenty minutes and two buses jammed to the window glass had passed. She said she would spend the night at her parents' home nearby and trudged off into the adjacent field of volcanic ash and vines. The Albanian eventually rode with us at my indulgence and expense because the taxi-driver was of a mind to be charitable with my tab.

We had been to visit Yeoryios Roussos, the owner of an old family winery, Canava Roussos, and my daughter was miffed when he drove down to the intersection in a truck from the winery, waved goodbye to us again and sped off in the direction going away from Fira, thus leaving us, she said, for the vultures. She also rebuked me for frittering away time on Santorini by visiting wineries. Not being a wine drinker she had no appreciation of Roussos. Santorini to him is a geological puzzlement that compels expression through the taste of wine – and he has made wines that leave my senses hanging fire over the edge of the caldera. Just to have the chance to chat with him on my previous visit I spent three hours one afternoon ambling up and down the black stone beach of Kamari waiting for Roussos to return from a funeral. The experience apparently left me with the sangfroid by which to let Santorini unfold over me in its own good time.

*

An acquaintance in New York who is a frequent visitor to Santorini recommended a *taverna* on the beach behind the airport near Kamari. The *taverna* is called Tomato and its kitchen is in a building that was once part of a tomato processing plant. It was already dark the evening I took my daughter to Tomato, and we mistakenly opened a door from which voices were emanating and walked into another building that had been part of the former tomato facility. The occupants were less than amused and pointed us firmly in the right direction.

You never know where Santorinian families will seek shelter. Indeed ekistics is the ultimate expression of the native genius for coping with the spectacular environment. A whole segment of the tourism industry is based on this today. It is centered at Oia, the village at the northern extremity of the island, where many visitors pay dearly to do without modern amenities in otherwise abandoned old dwellings. Personally, I prefer the inland villages on the southern portion of the plain. Several of these villages have the appearance of warrens and from some angles give the impression of being actually embedded in the landscape. I had set aside the last day of our visit to be free of wineries and to take my daughter to explore Messaria, Pyrgos or Megalochorio, but her acquaintance with local architecture came to a premature end after the bowl of tomatoes she polished off the day before at the evocatively traditional showplace Boutari winery. She was incapacitated on our final day.

I had visited Megalochorio on my earlier visit when one of the elderly Gavalas brothers, who was selling the family wines on tap in Athens, suggested that I visit his brother, the wine maker, who at the time was at the family home in the village for Easter. Megalochorio is a compound in which one cubic dwelling blends anonymously into the next, and I never would have found the Gavalas home without the help of a man I encountered once I was deep within the confines of the commune. Lanes seemed to bend too frequently for me either to get a fix on where I might be going or to keep track of where I already had been.

The wine maker Gavalas and his wife graciously invited me in for *visanto* and cookies. They had not been to bed owing to the Easter celebration, but they were glad for the visit as soon as I told them that the brother in Athens had sent me. The home was built of pumice stone in the centuries-old Santorini fashion and was virtually impervious to any weather extremes that might be felt outdoors. Next door was a similar structure that served as the wine cellar. Gavalas took me there to taste several more wines. He explained the local wine traditions and predicted they would go down the drain after his generation was gone. A reddish dry wine of his that I would gladly have taken off his hands barrel and all, if I could have managed it, helped me get over that thought.

*

Genuine elements of folk culture have become hard to spot beneath all the tourist clutter. On my first visit I engaged a room on the plain at a brand-new hotel that was folksy in décor but occupied solely by Athenians at least one generation removed from folksiness, who at the time of my checking in, late in the evening, were massing to process to a church for the Easter liturgy. I waited out the liturgy but joined the returning celebrators, all bearing their lit Easter candles in hand, for the traditional *mayeritsa* soup of lamb entrails and greens. The proud new hotel-owner and his wife were caught up in the spirit of the occasion and entertained all of us with an impromptu *ballos*, a Cycladic jig for couples.

The first thing I noticed upon arrival in Fira on the visit with my daughter was an eatery with the unpromising name 'Macedonia.' To our relief we later found that several chi-chi restaurants were now dedicated to preserving the local foodstuffs and flavors and were able to sell fava as manna. Most of their clientele were non-natives who long to look as leathery as the old Santorinian men who, aboard their donkeys, have been pushed to the side of the road by the beach-bound buses. At one of these restaurants I ate a fava-and-pork *terrine* that would be a hit in the Hamptons or Malibu. Santorini's cooking traditionally tended to be arid because the island can support no olive trees.

My daughter's closest brush with old island culinary ways was *pseftokeftethes* ('pseudo-meatballs'), the meatless fried patties that the Santorinians concoct from various vegetable sources. Of course the most characteristic kind of patty is one made from fava and dried dwarf tomatoes, whose austere texture can be counteracted by tomatoes served in the fresh state, although a judicious helping of both is advisable lest, as happened to my daughter, one is undone by them.

We had several encounters with *pseftokeftethes* during our visit. Even Roussos offered them at his winery. He had expanded his operations beyond wine in the years since my first visit and was serving *mezethes* to winery visitors. He was also presenting costumed Greek folk dance performances. A dancer who spoke with us before the show was a lad from Central Greece and he was dressed in national rather than Santorinian costume. But we did not stay to watch. The musicians were warming up and they were playing national rather than Cycladic rhythms. I was sure there would be no *ballos* – just a surfeit of false-meatballs.

10

IN THE EYE OF THE BEHOLDER
(or "Yes, We Have No Bananas")

On about ten days each year the sun shines so brightly by my apartment along the Potomac that the sky takes on a sparkling clarity recalling the hallmark Aegean condition. I wait for those days the way some other people do eclipses and if at all possible arrange to enjoy a glass of wine on my riverside balcony at noontime. The appearance of the wine on those occasions rekindles in me a feel for the motivation that must have come to early Aegean wine growers through their eyes during the era when they were creating the wines that would become typical of their islands. But the experience always falls short of the start I had in eastern Crete the first time the ancient outlook was thrust on me.

Crete is, emphatically, a place for great things; smallness does not fit there. Nobody feels this more than the Cretans themselves: "For never will I shame the halls of Crete" (Phaedra's pledge in Euripides's *Hippolytus*). Native son Nikos Kazantzakis makes all this plain in his writings, above all in *Freedom or Death*, his novel about Crete's struggle to free itself from Ottoman rule. The heroic dimensions of Crete become keenly apparent when the story's protagonist, Captain Michalis, decides to throw one of his occasional eight-day-and-eight-night bacchanals of wine and sausage; and the tavern keeper Vendusos, obviously out of concern for the condition of Cretan halls, prays to My Lady of the Vineyard, "Help me to hold out and not to get drunk and not be sick this time, and make a mess of the walls." Crete indeed is a place to be reckoned with.

I booked passage on an overnight ferry from Piraeus to the Cretan capital of Iraklion. It was the first time I ever ate my evening meal aboard a Greek ferry and I celebrated the occasion by jettisoning my usual lunchtime order of 'ferryboat *pastitsio*' (a distinctive though demotic recipe that apparently is imparted to all ferryboat cook trainees at the national maritime service school). I ordered lamb chops instead. And in place of my usual *portokalada*, a fizzy orange drink, I ordered a bottle of manly Cretan white wine of the old school, which could hold its own with lamb. I was able to manage no more than half the bottle, but not being Cretan I did not take this poor performance as an affront to myself. And in any case I could at least pride myself on having kept the bulkheads clean and my cabin balmy.

We docked the next morning near the old Venetian fortress that gave Iraklion the name that Kazantzakis knew it by, Megalo Kastro (Great Fortress), which it bore through Venetian and Turkish times. It was hardly 7 o'clock in the morning but the sun was already high and the town active. On the advice of an agricultural cooperative's representative I took a bus to nearby Karteros, where the Canadian-trained Cretan owner of a hotel along the beach let me check into a room despite the irregular hour. I was back in Iraklion in time for the early queue at the Bank of Crete's foreign exchange window.

I spent the better part of the day kicking around town and trying mentally to reconstruct Kazantzakis's Megalo Kastro. I would especially have liked to conjure Captain Michalis and the cast of characters he would round up for his force-feedings. The best I could do, however, was when I came upon an old cutlery shop with a large signboard picturing a traditionally garbed Cretan *pallikari*, a 'brave,' sporting one of the characteristic long knives – or short swords, depending on how one sizes it up – that have come in handy in ridding the island of all occupiers save those who arrive nowadays with valises and backpacks, against whom the Cretans have devised no offense.

Speaking of the great and the small, these outmoded Cretan weapons cut to the heart, or rather to the nether side, of the aggrieved gravity of Crete. The Cretan male's preoccupation with knives grew out of a huge mistake made by his Minoan forefathers during the island's phallic worship period. Delighting in themselves, those early Cretans liked to make statues featuring 'the male parts,' rather as a perpetual reminder to Minoan women of the crucial male role. The upshot was statues with exaggerated phalluses, and ultimately the worship of bulls, all of which apparently stimulated the imagination of some Minoan women. One of them, Pasiphaë by name, developed a crush on a particularly handsome bull and arranged to achieve coition with him by having herself placed inside a specially constructed model of a cow. (The outcome of the dubious liaison was the Minotaur, who had the horns and body of a bull but the head and torso of a man; and who dwelt in the famed Labyrinth, where he regularly devoured sacrificial children until Theseus came and slew him.) Cretan men have never fully recovered psychologically from Pasiphaë's perfidy, which they take as a mocking sign of her dissatisfaction with them. They have labored long centuries to rehabilitate their image in the eyes of Cretan women – though apparently, judging from all the blue eyes to be seen amongst the island populace, without any great success.

The classical Minoan anxiety festered like an open wound in the taxi-driver, Sarandos, who took me out to eastern Crete. I had run into him my first evening in Iraklion. Or rather, he had nearly run me over. I had just dropped off several chance English companions at their hotel, and as I stepped off the curb in front of the entrance I was almost hit by a taxi, whose driver was Sarandos. Taking me for a local, he unleashed a torrent of invective from behind the windshield, all to tell me to watch where the hell I was going. But once I stepped around to the driver's window to ask about a ride back to Karteros and Sarandos understood that I was not from these parts, he became apologetic about

Greek Salad

having got in my way. And when, on the way out to the hotel, I asked him where I could catch a bus heading east the next day, Sarandos recommended that I avoid the hassle, save time and hire him for the excursion. With presence worthy of Phaedra, he pledged punctuality, reliability and honesty. Letting bygones be bygones, I engaged him.

Sarandos was parked in front of the hotel the next morning before I had even wiped the sleep from my eyes. Eastward, ho! to Sitia, a little port town nearly at the end of the island. Crete is older than Greece, and some of the oldest evidence of grapevine cultivation has been unearthed out Sitia way. Sitian red wine was of special interest to me because it is made from a grape of certifiable Minoan origin and I had never, not even in Iraklion the day before, been able to find any of it.

Sarandos was frankly indifferent about wine. What fired him up, I soon found out, was bananas. The fact that Crete grows bananas was a point of great pride with Sarandos. We even stopped en route to Sitia so he could show me what he said was the only plantation of banana trees on the island's northern coast; most Cretan bananas dangle to the south towards Africa. I could have thought the banana tree is where Cretan machismo has had to take refuge since the sheathing of knives, except that I already knew the bananas Crete grows are a dwarf kind much disparaged by Athenians. The subject of Cretan bananas was topical in Athens at that time, in the early 1980s, because the Greek government, under pressure from Cretan growers, had banned imports of *real* bananas. (It was a singular coincidence that on my return ferry trip from Iraklion to Piraeus a Greek couple visiting from overseas was aboard with their playful pet chimpanzee. I neglected to ask about his reaction to the Cretan growths.)

Seaside scenery gradually gave way to mountainous country not long after the road from Iraklion was met by the road coming north from the banana country around Ierapetra facing Africa. As we began to climb, white villages were to be seen strung out along blunt ridges, with hillside vineyards appearing in profusion all around. We arrived shortly at Exo Mouliana and took a break at a café. Inside we found the usual collection of elderly men who congregate in such establishments at mid-morning. These Cretans were armed with nothing more threatening than canes. The men were more than glad to talk about wine, and one of them informed me with obvious pride that Lucullus himself had been a devoted customer for Sitian wine (Cretan men can, as I indicated, harbor painfully long memories). Another one, a pensioner who hobbled as a result of injuries received during the German occupation of Crete in the Second World War, volunteered that he was making some of the local red wine, and he invited me to his cellar for a glass of it. I left with him while Sarandos remained at the café.

Greek Salad

We were at the cellar in no time. I waited in an ante-room while the grower went further in for the wine. As he returned I took the offered glass from his extended hand and he immediately grasped me firmly by the elbow to urge me out of the semi-darkness and into the day. In the light shadow of the whitewashed cellar I stood looking at the wine against a background of white afforded by the next village over. But I went even further and did what is unthinkable to the modern enologist – I stepped into the dazzling sunlight with my glass. My eyes reeled in disbelief at the furious reddish orange gleam that struck them. I had to think that the ancient Greeks would have described Sitian wine as *pyrros*, or 'flame-colored,' a term they liked to use because of its association with the sun, and indeed with vision itself, Plutarch having written that vision is dependent on the 'flame-like' (*pyrodi*) brilliance of the sun. Certainly while looking at Sitian wine that first time I felt transported back to sunup in the epoch of Aegean wine.

Mundaneness must have come over me upon reentering the cellar, because my next thought was to ask the pensioner whether the villagers have preferences about what foods to eat with their wine. I had been so taken by its color that I could imagine them being appreciative of it with virtually anything; although, under the influence of its very color, I personally might have taken a visual tack and leaned toward golden brown foods that Greeks describe as 'reddish.' The pensioner told me that some villagers do indeed have preferences, but that they do not much agree in them. However the case might be, disks of local pork sausage, *loukaniko*, were being served up for the common good back in the café. I thought perhaps at least pork is universally enjoyed with the local wine since Crete has reveled in pork since remote times (and has the bones to prove it).

"Sin," wrote Kazantzakis in terms a Cretan would well understand, "should be a mountain of pork to be mastered, a lake of wine in which to swim – not just a tidbit." Freedom or death indeed. But the sausages at the café in Exo Mouliana were only average in size, like the ones Captain Michalis would ply the drunken weenies with at his cellar. Rosemary Barron, the British writer on Greek cookery, tells of a more fitting Cretan sausage, a rare but marvelous smoked *loukaniko* of one-meter length that gives rise to suggestive wisecracks whenever it makes a public appearance intact, before having lengths sliced off for use. Both the sausage and the wisecracks must go back to Pasiphaë's time. And it may be supposed that it really takes a Cretan to savor all the pathos of the vignette in Kazantzakis's *Zorba the Greek* in which the freshly neutered pig seems to have a beastial comprehension of the nature of the delicacy being enjoyed in the farmyard by his owner and the honored guests. At any rate, the café scene I played in, with my glass of Sitian wine still in hand, was all of Kazantzakis's Crete that I was going to get.

Greek Salad

Sarandos and I continued on from Exo Mouliana and went all the way down to Sitia town, where we repaired to a *taverna* for lunch. In the expansive spirit of Crete I threw caution to the wind and ordered a bottle of Sitian red wine with grilled fish. In looking at this phenomenal wine again I remembered an apt detail in the closing scene of the film version of *Zorba the Greek*, as Zorba and the young owner of the lignite mine sit on the beach and eat spit-roasted lamb and drink wine. Zorba takes in his hand a glass of the wine and casts at it what Kazantzakis called his "primordial glance which seizes its nourishment arrow-like from on high." The wine, the sun, the brilliant clarity, the pebbles throwing back the rays through the glass and into Zorba's ready eyes and soul – all seem to make up the eternal Aegean scene, older than the ancients' notion of an alliance of fire, sun and wine, yet fresher than the words of a modern Greek popular song, "I want you to be an eagle, that the light of the sun be your wine." I could imagine Zorba dashing an enologist's instruments onto the pebbles, shaking him by the shoulders and telling him to throw away his data and really *see* the wine. I was profoundly grateful in that moment that Sitian red wine had been brought into being in an age when a Zorba would take his wine out to look at it in the light of his place.

Sarandos, however, had greater, Cretan matters on his mind. "We used to get big bananas on Crete," he swore. "But now we don't get them anymore. I don't know what happened." Obviously he was not familiar with Greek banana politics. The big bananas Sarandos remembered were actually the imported ones that the Greek government in the meantime had banned, not the Cretan ones. It seemed to me that the only satisfactory resolution of the issue would have to be Freudian. Maybe the Cretans could plant more cucumbers. But I was not sure how to express this take on it intelligibly and without insult in Greek. Besides, Sarandos otherwise was so perfectly content with his life on Crete that I did not want to disturb his bliss by informing him of the awful truth about Cretan bananas.

11

COCKADOODLEDOO!!

The tourist season was winding down and natives of the eastern Aegean islands were preponderant on the ferry from Piraeus to Samos one late September day. A disproportionately large share of the embarkees were well along in years, the explanation for which turned out to be Ikaria, Samos's western neighbor and the ferry's first destination. Emigration by its economically active population had left Ikaria, in effect, a retirement community. Some of the Ikarians on the ferry were so old as to seem beyond the aging process and bore the most wizened countenances I have seen in the Aegean. Most of the relatively few foreigners on the ferry also were elderly people headed for Ikaria. The island's radium-charged thermal waters are sometimes recommended by physicians in western Europe.

I was out on deck among a collection of Ikarian men for the better part of the nine-hour voyage as far as their island. The day was a lark for them and they filled it with a lot of good-humored banter. Their womenfolk provided a flat contrast. Clad in the perpetual mourning garment of rustic Greek women old enough to have seen many of their immediate relatives die off, most of the Ikarian women had scrambled for the vessel's indoor benches as soon as they boarded. They apparently had made up their minds to achieve seasickness, which they in fact managed to do before we sailed out of the Saronic Gulf past Cape Sounion and into open water. Struck that an ancient maritime folk could not commonly know that the cure for gathering seasickness is in getting out into the weather, I thought how sweet, though how dearly justified, a whole day spent on their hips must come to them.

I had no realization of it at the time, but I was somewhat infirm myself when I boarded the ferry. I had been drifting too far on the Vinous Sea. Zorba advised total immersion as the only cure for hankerings, such as mine to understand wine, but I was forgetting to come up for air. I was in danger of drowning in a variety of compulsions that I mistook for free choice. Going to Samos was itself symptomatic of my condition. The island's name is practically synonymous with sweet Muscat, and I could not rest easy until I decided for myself about its ranking among wines. I was spurred by the comment of a 19th century French visitor who reckoned, rather too indefinitely for my taste, that if Samian Muscat wines "are not deserving of being placed in the first rank, they can occupy the second without much handicap." I wanted to know just how good Samos Muscat could be, and going to the source seemed the best way to find out.

The ferry was to make two stops at Samos, the first at Karlovassi on the northwestern coast and the second on the northeastern coast at Vathy, the island capital. I had planned on staying in Vathy because the main offices of the wine cooperative EOSS are located there. However, two ship's stewards persuaded me to disembark at Karlovassi instead. They were living there and praised it as "more open" than Vathy, by which I understood them to mean less compactly settled. In fact, from what I could see of the place when we arrived, which was after nightfall, Karlovassi struck me as an awkward, straggling, semi-urban agglomeration having no center of gravity. But it seemed to have all the essentials for someone who was not backpacking, and the clerk at the hotel to which I was directed offered me a room that he said had a seaward view. Insofar as Aegean ports of call were concerned, I was feeling quite comfortable about the second rank.

One of the stewards had put me in the hands of a taxi-driver friend of his, Vangeli, who took me to the hotel. Vangeli and I ended up striking an agreement whereby he would also chauffeur me around while I was on Samos. With his work at an end for the day, as it always is after the last ferry arrives, we settled in at a table at O Pittas grill near the hotel to clinch our agreement over a bottle of dry Muscat wine and a platter of pork *souvlaki*. I sat half listening to him tell me about the financial distress of grape growers and half evaluating the wine (it was a compulsion after all). He spoke of farmers at the mercy of what he habitually and derisively referred to as "the little people" of Samos, a category in which he lumped together bankers, priests and EOSS managers, all of whom, he alleged, were in cahoots to keep the peasants in thrall. Vangeli warmed to his subject and soon expanded to the worldwide plight of farmers. He spoke with such genuine emotion that I was riveted as I had not been by speakers at a world food conference I once attended.

Vangeli had little faith in 'rich' Samos. His earliest memories were of the Second World War, and mostly what he remembered was great want. He had a younger brother who died of malnutrition during the war. Meanwhile, as he was speaking, Vangeli noticed the cats patiently eyeing our food as if they knew from long experience at O Pittas that some of it was bound to be theirs eventually. He grasped up the piece of a bread loaf he knew we would never finish, slammed it down on the table and demanded to know how it can be that something so precious to people as bread can be so cheap as to be left for cats, while so many of the world's farmers, like the grape growers of Samos, barely eke out a living. Suddenly I felt ashamed submitting the satisfying wine to the fine discrimination of my critical faculty.

If it had not been for Vangeli and our agreement I would not have lasted in Karlovassi past the first night. From 10 p.m. until around midnight the bump-car amusement ride located on the lot between O Pittas and the hotel was doing a land-office business, and the fact that the Samians had not acquired the hang of aggressiveness behind the wheel made no dent in the decibel level. About midnight, however, a changing of the guard took place, with motorcycles replacing the bump-cars as the source of noise. Wherever the center of Karlovassi is, the hotel apparently marked the settlement's outer limits, because at that point, just after a bend in the road, a straight stretch of pavement invited every lunatic on two motor-driven wheels to step on the gas with all the fanfare that could be coaxed from their engines – and none turned down the invitation. That audio show lasted until 2 a.m., which I noted by glancing from the supine at my propped up watch on the nightstand. Only then did urban Karlovassi call it a day. But not to be outdone, rural Karlovassi began to crow around 4 a.m. The roosters evidently succeeded in rousing construction laborers, because by 5:30 work was all too audibly underway on the new hotel that was going up across the way (and obstructing, I now noticed, my view to the sea). By this time I could not deny to myself the error in having gone with Number Two.

Vangeli took me to meet Samians great and small. We started in Karlovassi at the Agricultural Bank, whose manager Vangeli caustically interrogated about the difficulty grape growers have getting loans for plumbing and other amenities. The issue took a human form afterward when we stopped along the road to give a lift to an old friend of Vangeli's who just that year had decided to throw in the towel on grape growing and found a better way to make ends meet through tourism. The man's complaint was about EOSS's practice of paying the bigwigs' salaries first while stringing growers along on unpredictable piecemeal payments. The installments were so erratic and small that even the Agricultural Bank was shy to lend to these agriculturalists.

We drove along the coastal road to Vathy, where Vangeli left me in the hands of another Agricultural Bank manager and his assistant. The manager had volunteered to drive me back to Karlovassi himself. He had been alerted to my visit by a phone call from a high-level official of the Bank whom I had met in Athens and told about my plans to visit Samos and EOSS. The manager now phoned EOSS to tell them we would be coming directly, and at their offices we found the topmost layer of management already assembled. I conducted a group interview while sipping choice 25-year-old Samian Muscat that certainly was in the upper stratum of the second rank of wines if not in the lower stratum of the first.

There was something peculiar about the Vathy bank manager. I spent nearly seven hours in his company and not the slightest trace of a smile passed over his face in all that time. At EOSS I behaved only like the harmless admirer of Samian wine that I was, but the more I revealed prior knowledge of Samos the more woeful the manager appeared. He was downright morose during lunch at a village *taverna*, and looked physically ill when the assistant, who stayed with us through lunch, abruptly shifted the conversa-

Greek Salad

tion away from Samos and mounted a gratuitous and hostile tirade on the subject of U.S.-Greece relations, which had recently plunged to a new low on the initiative of Greek Prime Minister Andreas Papandreou.

After dropping off his assistant at the bank, the manager took me on a drive inland into vine-clad mountains. We went by way of a road that took us from Mediterranean to Middle European scenery and from summer to fall weather all at once, and I had the manager stop a number of times so I could take photographs of the countryside and village life. Later, on the road to Karlovassi, he stated bleakly that he had not been able to determine exactly what sorts of subjects I like to photograph but that to him it seemed my preference was for scenes of delapidation. From this comment he went directly into a request that I send him some postcards from Washington, D.C., for his postcard collection he said, and give him my home address in case he ever visited. I had no time to respond before he looked at me nervously and wondered aloud whether he was inconveniencing me.

I met up with Vangeli again that evening at O Pittas. He laughed with great delight when I told him all about my hours with 'the little people.' The explanation for the behavior of my hosts in Vathy was transparent to him. According to Vangeli, the manager and the assistant suspected that interest in Muscat wine was only my cover to gain their confidence, and that I had really been sent by the Papandreou government to investigate agricultural affairs on Samos. Vangeli explained that the bank manager was a pre-Papandreou appointee who was afraid for his future, while the assistant was a Papandreou appointee out to make a politically correct impression. A malicious grin spread across Vangeli's face as he suggested I drop both of them discomfiting notes from Athens and use as a return address that of either the Agricultural Bank or the Ministry of Agriculture.

The next morning our destination was the high-country and (in universal Samian estimation) first-rank wine village of Platano. A friend of Vangeli's at the café on the village *plateia* brought some Muscat wine from a local grape grower, which we sipped pleasurably until the quiet of the square was shattered by the sound of a Greek army truck backing into the front end of Vangeli's parked taxi. Vangeli had spent six years in the Belgian Congo accumulating his fortune, such as it was, invested in his taxi and home. He rained such terrible verbal abuse on the private who was driving the truck that the young man surely would have preferred one of his sergeant's sweet melodies.

The commotion brought Platano's mayor out onto the *plateia*, and he came to sit with us after the dust had settled. The mayor had his walking stick in hand and his jacket slung cape-like over his shoulders, and in general exuded self-importance. He was followed a few minutes later by a gray-bearded priest who happened to be his brother-in-law. The mayor and the priest sang the merits of Platano for me, the foreigner, and would have had me believe they were personally responsible for all of it. Vangeli tapped me ever so discretely on the finger as if to signal, "Just listen to all of this stuff."

After Vangeli made a last inspection of his taxi's bruise and muttered some more, we departed the *plateia* and took a road out to an area of vineyard terraces. He now vented his more specific views on Samian priests, who would, he said, come out and bless a brothel if moneyed patrons called them out to do it. We stopped when he spotted a pickup truck he recognized. Nearby we found its sun-browned owner working like a navvy to construct a new terrace. His wife joined us not long afterward and the four of us drove to another vineyard of theirs, where in the shade of a grape arbor next to their tool shed we enjoyed an impromptu lunch of bread, goat cheese, and olives, as well as tomatoes and muscat grapes right off the vines. Water was our only drink.

The couple said their financial situation had become very tight because one of their daughters had just married and the new household had to be put on its feet. At the same time, the year's grape harvest, which was already in progress in vineyards at lower altitudes where the fruit ripens earlier, was the worst in memory in both quality and quantity. The family could no longer afford to hire laborers to help in the vineyards. Gazing out at a first-rate view of Samos and the Aegean, I thought that being a Samian grape grower must have a bright side. I asked the couple whether they ever get down to the seaside below in the distance, but they responded only with mute puzzlement, and Vangeli jibed, "They bathe only in their own sweat."

Vangeli and I parted company the next day when he dropped me off at a hotel he knew on the waterfront of Pythagorion, a fishing and yachting port on the southeastern coast of Samos facing Asia Minor. I wasted no time in heading for the sea. I also took my lunch break at the *taverna* on the beach, where I ordered a bottle of Samian rosé at a price that was not going to do Samian winegrowers any good. It was too much wine for me and I ended up sharing it with a German woman named Helga who had sat down at a neighboring table right after me. This led to a lingering conversation.

Helga was an engaging talker and raconteur. Some of her stories were hilarious, like the one about how she had lost her way while motorbiking on Samos and ended up down a vineyard path where an elderly grape grower exposed himself to her. I found myself oddly sympathetic about his bacchic antics because I was sure from everything I had heard in the preceding days that he was not getting any other jollies in the vines.

There was also a Zorba-esque side to Helga in that she confronted things straight on without getting lost

Greek Salad

in superfluous considerations and questions. She was somewhat impatient with those of us who make life difficult by letting sundry complexities interpose themselves and obscure simple essentials. It was just in that vein that she teased me about my interest in wine and told me, only half jokingly, "everyone must find some way to kill themselves," by which she meant what Zorba did when he said that everyone has his own paradise (Zorba always said that he would be finished off by his, women). She smirked and shook her head as if to say, "Will you never learn?!" And I guess she thought I would not, because she leaned in flirtatiously and asked if I was still thinking about wine. It was a wake-up call for me.

The next day, my last on Samos, I felt as though the peculiar staleness attendant upon compulsions had slipped off me, and I went for a swim to complete the mood of a cleansing. As I sat on the beach surrounded by people trying to divest themselves of as much material covering as they felt comfortable without, I was surprised by the sight of an old Samian man dressed from head to toe as if for late autumn, although it was still only September, and a very warm one at that. He was trudging through the sand with sacks in his hands. I thought perhaps he was a public servant assigned to keep the beach clean, but he turned out to be peddling fruits of the season. From me he went on to others, and he was not in the least distracted by the baubles of breasts as he earnestly offered his grapes and figs.

Aegean Islands

The Samian's whole appearance and manner struck me so comically that I could hardly contain my laughter as I kept my eye on his path down the beach. I had to be on my way for another ferry ride, but I started laughing so hard I could scarcely walk through the sand. It was a most free laugh, and it caught me off guard. I think I had not heard it in such an awfully long time. I realized then that it is only with a considerable handicap that wine can occupy the second rank of life's enjoyments.

12

KISSES SWEETER THAN WINE

I was still young when I went to Chios. But I was already a confirmed winebibber, and wine, or at least wine history, could have supplied plenty of reason for going. No vintage of antiquity was more touted than was the Chian. It even fostered the earliest recorded instance of unabashed wine snobbery. A nobleman by the name of Demetrius was brought before a court on charges of profligacy, and he thought to impress the judges by dragging the reputation of Chian wine into the defense of his own. His statement at the proceedings was quoted by Athenaeus in *The Deipnosophists*:

> "But I am living as becomes a man of breeding as it is. For I have a mistress fair, I have never wronged any man, I drink Chian wine, and in all other respects I contrive to satisfy myself."

Yet it was not wine that motivated my visit. I chose Chios on a whim having to do, instead, with fair mistresses. I was in Salonika on a September day during the period of the city's annual international trade fair and could find no accommodations downtown, not even through the tourist police. Figuring to sleep with the Aegean as my box spring, I decided to see if any ships were departing for the islands that evening. A travel agent presented several sailings and destinations, and my sole reference in choosing Chios was a witty Greek folk song that came to mind when the island's name was mentioned. The song, 'A Boat from Chios,' claims that the kisses of Chian women are like no others, a proposition that I, as a wine lover attuned to the distinctions implicit in geographical names, was prepared to entertain. Prices in an unstated currency are quoted in the lyrics of the song: four for the kisses of a married woman, and fourteen for those of a widow (and I had wondered that Zorba prized widows!), while those of a maiden were to be had for the price of a joke. Having as yet more interest in romance than wine, I daydreamed of uncovering a Greece of untethered women and running into a helluva time on Chios. Not having Demetrius's means for profligacy, I hoped that the price ratios mentioned in the old song had held up, and I expected that at any rate maidens might still fall within the possibilities of my resources.

The ferry voyage, however, laid me up my first day on Chios. I had drunk water from the pitcher that was secured to the wall of my cabin, without stopping to think of the number of sailings that the bacteria in the pitcher might have made. I did not leave the hotel all day. It was my birthday, too, and a helluva way to spend it. By evening I was up to lounging in the lobby, where I had a conversation with a German guest who had already been on Chios a week. He informed me that the Greek army had recently settled in on Chios en masse in the wake of the Turkish occupation of Cyprus. Passions more violent than kissing might be unleashed because of Cyprus, and the Turks might attempt to ferry across from Asia Minor to stage a repeat of their 1822 Chian massacre.

Sand being fertile for flirtations, the first excursion I made on Chios the next day was to a beach south of town that the German had mentioned. I set off on foot and followed a road through the eastern coastal plain facing Turkey across the channel. Not too far out of town a promising vista attracted me to a seaward path. But several children coming toward me along the road started shouting "*Narkes*!" and pointing to a field behind a fence ahead of me. My Greek was weak on military terminology and I needed the children's imitations of explosions before I put two and two together and realized that they meant land mines. I now had tangible reason to think that world politics might cramp my style. I wished that the travel agent in Salonika had let me know that Chios might any day become a battleground.

Signs spelling out *ΝΑΡΚΕΣ* were displayed from that point to several kilometers further south, until the road ran alongside a long tract of sand. The beach was not mined and the snack shop was open for business, but neither maidens nor matrons were to be seen. I concluded that I could not have chosen a less propitious time to go a-mashing on Chios. Hope shimmered like a mirage as I emerged from a dip and made out a trio of Nereids taking up a position near the shack and not far from where my towel was spread. But I lost all interest in their kisses as soon as I determined they were not Chian women (geographical origin is of the essence to the wine lover). The several Chian men populating the shack were of a different mind and began coming out on the porch by turns, as though standing lookout watch against the Turks, to peek at all that these Nordic peacekeeping forces were baring as they bivouacked on the beach. A strange way to behave, I thought, for men who should have no reason to look for kisses other than the famed ones they already get. Tourism evidently was turning their heads so far that they had lost sight of the old song I knew.

Wanting to see as much of Chios as possible in case I never sailed that way again, I took a bus the next day to the southern end of the island, to the village of Piryi. Visitors usually go to Piryi either for its 12th century church or for the facades of its buildings, which are covered with the geometric designs called *xysta*, or 'scratchings.' After poking around in the church several minutes I decided that it was not for me. Nor am I the sort to find greater than average fascination in a folk putterer's isosceles fantasies. Once I began suffering flashbacks to high school geometry class and a disastrous class project, I took off down an unscratched medieval lane that eventually led into a Gethsemane of disorderly olive and mastic trees where I was able to exchange a Euclidean frame of reference for Theophrastean thoughts on plant smells.

Greek Salad

A sturdy ploughman type who was sitting on a bench in the lane through which I passed had alerted me to the presence of the sturdy little mastic trees, which anywhere else I might have thought were just overgrown bonsais. He was hunched giant-like over a pile of tiny mastic crystals and was cleaning them for market. He said that mastic is Piryi's cash crop and has been exported for centuries, and I remembered seeing 'Chian mastic' listed on old apothecary inventories at Colonial Williamsburg. The Greeks used to chew the aromatic mastic to sweeten their breath. With Chios being the world's major source of mastic, the Chians of pre-toothpaste times must have enjoyed a mouth-to-mouth advantage, even if Williamsburg was never celebrated in American colonial song as a hotbed of kisses.

I roamed freely in the grove until I stopped to lift and bite a hardened droplet of mastic sap from the ground beneath the bushes. Shots rang out. I stood up immediately to see whether the Turks were closing in. But all I saw was a lone sentry standing guard over the crop from a distant lookout post. I knew I had overstayed my welcome in Piryi.

Still keen to try my luck on the sands, I left the hotel the next morning with my swimsuit and a towel again. I stopped at a grocery for some cheese and bread to take along and inquired from the grocer about beaches. Another customer overheard me and suggested I take a bus and try Kardamyla. He evidently had sympathy for me because of my American accent. Such sympathy was rare enough amongst the Greeks at that time because they saw a decidedly pro-Turkish tilt to American policy on Cyprus. The customer's helpfulness was explained when he went on to tell me that his wife was American. He also mentioned, with a tinge of Brahmin pride that must have been transmitted conjugally, that her ancestors had arrived in America aboard the *Mayflower*. He clearly knew to expect this information to have cultural import for me, and in a way it did: I wondered whether his wife might have retained an ancestral Early American memory of Chian mastic.

Kardamyla, being on the far northeastern coast, nicely suited my ambitious touring plans for Chios. I walked around the village a while without sighting any water, and wandered into a miniature Eden where I stole a pomegranate from a garden guarded only by an unconcerned goat. Shortly thereafter an old man set me in the direction of a beach, but only after he understood just what it was I was looking for (I had used the word *plaz*, which apparently was taken from French too recently for it to have reached his generation of Greek island villager). Not a soul was on the beach, but not necessarily because of the Turkish threat – plastic trash marked the high tide line and was off-putting. I moved on and hiked to a promontory where an attractive white chapel stood, and on the coast below I found a secluded spot where the dips of the tourist brochures are had.

Greek Salad

Three soldiers were awaiting the Turkish invasion in a defunct windmill I passed on my way back into the village later on. I stopped to chat on the impulse that they might have something encouraging to tell me about Chian women, but instead they complained that chaperoning was the order of the day. Their report was confirmed by another soldier who was sitting on the bench beside the village bus stop while I was waiting to return to town. He pointed out a lass accompanied by her brother on the menacing mission of purchasing vegetables that were being sold from the back of a truck. The Greek army may have been trying to keep a low profile, but the Chians were acutely aware of the uniformed presence anyway and taking extra precautions to keep their maidens out of range of jokes that might coax a kiss.

My last two days on Chios were spent in the northwestern part of the island. On the western coast north of Volissos, Chios rises in rugged contrast to the east and the south. The mountains separating the northwest from the northeast are high enough that clouds coming over from Asia Minor in winter can drop heavy snows on the northwest (Pausanias related that Chios got its name from the Greek word for snow, *chioni*). But it was only September, and in Volissos a shopkeeper told me about the virtues of various Chian fruits. He let me sample table grapes that he said came from the village of Kourounia further north. But Kourounia, he emphasized, is more famous for wine.

Aegean Islands

Having all but given up on Chian kisses, I decided to visit Kourounia and try the smack of Chian wine.

I learned from the villagers of Kourounia, ingloriously named in modern times for its pigs (*gourounia*), that the wine which earned Chios its fame anciently, Ariousian, was the product of their steep slopes by the island's northern coast.   Kourounia's vineyards, though, were a sad sight. The ancient vineyards of Ariousia were obliterated by the Turks in 1822 and the place never managed to get back on its vine stumps afterward. Used to basking in the certain continuity of the 20th century's renowned wine regions, I felt an eerie discomfort in looking at the few patches of vines that now dotted Kourounia's slopes.

I was able to find a villager who was still drawing off a few amphoras of latter-day Ariousian wine from his vines every year, and he gave me a glass of a dark red one made from partially raisined grapes. Athenaeus mentioned dry, semi-sweet and sweet Ariousian wines. I had to think that what I was tasting was the descendant of the semi-sweet kind, but the ancients did not leave behind wine tasting notes sufficiently detailed that I might make a more certain identification. The wine maker's wife reminisced about an especially successful cask of it decades earlier, in the prime of her life, and said, in finest rustic Greek idiom, "When you kissed after drinking it, it was 'all cinnamon and nutmeg'." Mastic obviously had never been needed at

Greek Salad

Kourounia, nor, we might suppose, at ancient Ariousia.

I ruefully watched the Turkish coast from the taffrail of the ferry for Piraeus the next evening and reflected on my Chian experiences. I may or may not have tasted an Ariousian wine like the one that the ancient nobleman Demetrius knew, but it was sure that I was never going to know whether or not the lyrics of the old song have any truth in them. I had no jolly songs to sing on 'the boat from Chios.'

PART II

MAINLAND GREECE

MAINLAND GREECE

(13) Epirus
(14) Siatista
(15) Naoussa
(16) Rapsani
(17) Larissa
(18) Pelion
(19) Arachova
(20) Athens
(21) Nafplion
(22) Patras

13

A DIFFERENT DRUMMER

Four steps to the right, two steps to the left. That's basically all there is to Greek politics. And to the *tsamiko*. But as the native folk dances go, the *tsamiko* moves at a snail's pace. It comes by its measure honestly, though, because it is first of all a regional dance rather than a national one. The region concerned is Epirus, an outlying breeding ground of eccentricity if ever Greece has had one. Epirus lies in the far northwestern corner of mainland Greece, just below Albania, and in fact the *tsamiko*'s name is attributed to an Epirote tribe known as the Chams.

Not everyone's bio-rhythms are geared to the *tsamiko*. And whether one characterizes it as doleful or stately probably depends mostly on where one's metabolism stands on it. As it happens, I have always felt a strong constitutional pull toward the *tsamiko*, so much so that I am inclined to think Epirote wine should also have a special appeal to me. For as the cognoscenti of these matters are quick to point out, regional arts and crafts and foods and wines spring from the same spirit and beat with the same pulse.

At one time, however, the thought of going to Epirus for wine never would have crossed my mind. Where the palate was concerned the only connection I made with the region was cheese. The Epirote lyrical idiom had also influenced me to think that way because it is more distinctly pastoral than any other in Greece. Or at least I cannot imagine another Greek region where a song would begin by noting that "the hour for milking" is at hand. Even when a gifted clarinetist coaxes the strains of a *tsamiko* to soar with the eagles, the lyrics do not go far above the heads of the sheep and goats. Wine does lend a lilt to the songs every now and then ("she offers us a golden cup of sweet wine"), but Epirus is the region where Byron's traveling companion Hobhouse observed wine being stored, like cheese, in goatskins with the hairy side turned inward, as though to ensure the savor everyone was most at home with.

Least of all could I have imagined ever going to Epirus for a cabernet sauvignon wine. For someone as given to the gait of the *tsamiko* as I am, cabernet could not seem any more in step with the region's aesthetic pace than the fox-trot is. But a report on the results of an international wine contest held in France landed on my desk at the U.S. Department of Agriculture one day in the early 1980s and showed an Epirote cabernet finishing remarkably well. Obviously this was not the same old Epirus I thought I knew. When I next returned to Greece I tried to find a bottle of the cabernet and update myself on Epirus, but I had no luck in finding one in Athens. I decided I might as well go to Epirus and at the same time get in touch with my terpsichorean homeland.

Mainland Greece

The cabernet came from the village of Metsovo high up in Byron's "bleak Pindus" mountains. But rather than take that rarefied air immediately, I first wanted to acclimate myself by breathing some heavier regional atmosphere down in the lower capital of Io-annina, the one-time citadel of Epirus's major histori-cal figure, Ali Pasha. Ali spat in the eye of the Otto-mans and ruled Epirus according to his own peculiar turn of mind – he was the Idi Amin of his day – for several decades in the late 18th and early 19th centu-ries. His appetite for everything from real estate on down to wine was on a grand scale. It cannot be mere coincidence that Ali repeatedly pestered places outside Epirus that were famous for their wine. Both Naoussa and Siatista across the Pindus in Macedonia, as well as Arachova in Central Greece, had to buy him off, rather in the way of paying 'protection money,' and it is on record that wine was among Ali's demands of them, his Moslem faith notwithstanding.

I caught a bus for Ioannina at the lagoon village of Mesolongi, famous as the place where Byron died of fever, in western Central Greece. The approach to Io-annina by that route, up the western side of the mainland, is undramatic, but it was the first time in Greece I had ever seen expanses of overgrown decidu-ous woods. Ioannina itself appeared from nowhere amidst the trees, its tattered fringe breaking Pan's spell. The town must have stuck out like a sore thumb in Byron's time too:

Greek Salad

Ne city's towers pollute the lovely view;
Unseen is Yanina, though not remote,
Veil'd by the screen of hills; here men are few,
Scanty the hamlet, rare the lonely cot:
But, peering down each precipice, the goat
Browseth; and, pensive o'er his scatter'd flock,
The little shepherd in his white capote
Doth lean his boyish frame along the rock,
Or in his cave awaits the tempest's short-lived
shock.

(*Childe Harold's Pilgrimage*)

Yet Ioannina was no mean place in those days. Its bazaar and other attractions exerted a strong tug on the sleeves of Epirote rubes, and many a capote was retired there:

I'm a beautiful shepherd girl,
A poor shepherd girl.
With the thousand sheep and five hundred goats,
That I guard from the wolves who'd eat them.
But I don't give a fig for the goats,
I'm leaving and off to Ioannina,
To the Bey's seraglio,
"Your health and happiness! Bey."

(Epirote folk song; *tsamiko*)

Nobody in Ioannina as far as I could tell was drinking cabernet, whether from Metsovo or anywhere else. It was not even listed on the restaurant and *tav-*

erna menus. Nor was it to be seen in grocery stores. The cabernet's absence hardly spoke of a budding regional wine tradition that might one day be choreographed by the local folk. I finally did manage to procure a bottle when I found what must have been Ioannina's only bona fide wine shop. But the cabernet was not decorating the shelves. The proprietor gingerly retrieved a sole bottle of the treasure from a drawer below the counter when I asked him about the Metsovo wine. I suddenly had the feeling I was in an exclusive jewelry shop, and actually, I had to pay for that bottle a price that seemed, at that time in Greece, a pasha's ransom. Adding palatal insult to pocket injury, when I opened it for a trial early that evening the contents made me wonder just how poorly wine stored afloat among goat hairs could fare.

But the evening was not a total loss. While walking about town at dusk I heard familiar musical sounds coming from a building situated near a park, and inside I found a wedding celebration in progress. It could have been a pan-Epirote jamboree, so many people were there. Uninvited guests were coming in off the street and standing freely beside the orchestra and dance floor. The music was regional and the dances more diverse than I knew them to be. But everything always came back to the *tsamiko*, and it was a splendid opportunity to see the special flair that native hoofers bring to it.

Greek Salad

Now, the casual observer looking at the *tsamiko* from outside the ring of dancers might see only a sodden dead march. However, the *tsamiko* in its way is a 'high-minded' dance, or at any rate it is upward in its motional orientation. Furthermore, nuances of footwork that the non-initiate will not spot are given ample time to creep in between the four steps to the right and the two to the left. When the dancers manage to synchronize the general well enough that the details can be articulated successfully, then the *tsamiko* can whisk you right out of your hide and give your soul wings in a way few other dances can. But that level of synergy is not achieved very often, at least not away from Epirus. For instance, at the Greek-American festivals where I usually dance the *tsamiko*, too many who join in are rooted in the boogie or the hustle or the jitterbug.

The wine being poured for the wedding guests was a sort of gavotte – an effervescent white wine. It came from the not too distant village of Zitsa, whose very name suggests the spritz the local wine has been famous for in Epirus ever since the secret of the technique was discovered by a fluke several centuries ago. Zitsa wine, either white or pink, and with varying amounts of bubbles, is also what sat on most tables at the *taverna* where I went for supper after sweating out my *tsamiko* fever. Since pink wine is the chief kind made around Zitsa, that was what I chose to drink with the spitted *splinantero* sausage of sheep and goat's blood that I ordered. The pink was semi-dry as well as semi-sparkling, which I am now convinced is what sheep's and goat's blood demands by way of counterpoint.

'Snap, crackle and pop' is, alas and alack, no *tsamiko* of a wine, but I modified my touring plans anyway and went directly to Zitsa instead of Metsovo the next day. Ali Pasha had not neglected Zitsa in his wine forages. In fact it was his favorite wine from his home territory, and the only person with whom he is known to have always maintained a civil relationship was the prior of the Monastery of the Prophet Elias, atop the hill above Zitsa, who took great pains with the fraternity's vineyards and wines. Ali even had his retreat in Zitsa, where he also preferred to entertain foreign guests, such as Byron. Hobhouse mentioned that the prior supplied wine for his and Byron's visit with Ali, and the bard himself alluded to this generosity in *Childe Harold's Pilgrimage*:

> Monastic Zitsa, from thy shady brow,
> Thou small, but favour'd spot of holy ground!
> Where'er we gaze, around, above, below,
> What rainbow tints, what magic charms are found!
> …
> The convent's white walls glisten fair on high:
> Here dwells the caloyer, nor rude is he,
> Nor niggard of his cheer; the passer by
> Is welcome still; nor heedless will he flee
> From hence, if he delight kind Nature's sheen to
> see.

Greek Salad

A secular winery was now operating not far below the abandoned monastery, and one of the owners was inside when I stopped by. He praised Zitsa's white wine for its "finesse" and gave me a taste of a barely carbonic one so fresh and light and dryly delicious that even a Rhinelander would have had to envy it. But I could not read any *tsamiko* features into this wine either. If the bubbly rosé performed a tarantella, the white did something of a polka, whereas the *tsamiko*, for all its lifts, does not quite get off the ground.

I drank a Zitsa white wine again at lunch the following day, which is remarkable only because I was in Metsovo. Not that I was entirely recovered from my first bout with the cabernet and ready to engage it again. But every wine deserves to be tried on its home turf; and besides, it would not have been cricket for me to fix my opinion of the cabernet based on a single sample which, because of its price alone, might have spent a year or more in a fusty drawer in a provincial town. But the restaurant did not stock the prestigious native growth. And this was despite the fact that Metsovo is a winter resort whose visitors generally can afford a pricey bottle.

I asked about the Metsovo winery at my hotel and was put in touch with Kosta Tritos, the manager of the village's commercial dairy. Kosta came to the hotel soon after and took me back to his home, where we sat on plumply cushioned furniture while his wife quietly served us cups of thick Turkish coffee and a silver tray of *kourabiethes*, or shortbread cookies, each fragrant from rose water and cloves and hidden under its own mound of confectioner's sugar. I felt myself the beneficiary of Levantine hospitality becoming a pasha. Yet by everything I knew of arts and crafts and foods and wines this pampered treatment seemed out of place in Metsovo's Alpine setting.

Kosta explained his involvement with the winery by informing me that it was another subdivision of the nonprofit foundation that was also operating the dairy. Of course he showed me around his own bailiwick first. He said the village's lactic traditions were steeped in ewe's milk and goat's milk but that the foundation had introduced milk cows in order to produce cheeses patterned after Italian prototypes. This could have been related to the adoption of the cabernet grape in Metsovo. For although the Metsovites might seem as tied to pasture as any other villagers in Epirus, they do have, as the cognoscenti of metaphysical gastronomy would note, something of a 'Latin' temperament. This temperament is transmitted by the Vlach language that the Metsovites speak in addition to Greek. Vlach, or Aromunian, is a holdover (like Romanian) from the time of Roman domination of the Balkan peninsula. But even so – and while I could never deny that Metsovo's cow's milk cheeses show that Latin steps can be danced there – my favorite cheese was the ewe's and goat's milk *chèvre*, which has, despite its Gallic nature, a special affinity for "bleak Pindus."

Greek Salad

In the office of the dairy, where the business aspects of the winery were managed, Kosta showed me the certificates that the Metsovo cabernet had won in various wine competitions, including the recent one that had sparked my curiosity about the village's vinous development. But Kosta was not the keeper of the keys to the winery itself and he had to phone another villager and ask him to meet us at the winery to let us in. This man, whose family was the only one in Metsovo that had managed to preserve a vineyard after the phylloxera pest attacked the village several decades earlier, told me that the native grape variety was a red one known as, appropriately enough, *vlahiko* (vlachian). Because of this apparent Latinate ethnic connection of the local grape, I could not suppose that *vlahiko* wine would be any more compatible than cabernet with the Illyrian cadence of the *tsamiko*. I was sure, though, that I would have preferred *vlahiko* to the vintages of cabernet that were on hand in the cellar, all of which reminded me, to a greater or lesser degree, of the bottle that had been unearthed for me in Ioannina. Not all the certificates in the world could paper over my disappointment.

Back down in Ioannina the next evening I was attracted to some oddly shaped brown bottles in a *taverna* so dim and dismal that Enver Hoxha's Albania could almost be felt breathing down Epirus's back. They looked like beer bottles, but the label identified the contents as wine. I was leery, and it must have registered on my face, because without my saying a word the elderly proprietor hurried to assure me that the wine was good. His expression was so guileless that all of my doubts were dispelled instantly and I confidently ordered a bottle with my meal.

The man at the winery below the old Zitsa monastery had mentioned a regional tradition of wine making that antedated the capture of carbonic gas, and said that someone in the neighboring village of Karitsa was bottling wine after that fashion commercially. But I had skipped Karitsa in order to hurry back to Ioannina and catch a bus for Metsovo. Yet it was just this wine from Karitsa, tasted in a miserable *taverna* in Ioannina, that restored my faith in the interconnection of arts and crafts and foods and wines. The Karitsan vintage was darkly pink and semi-sweet, as archaic in aspect as in texture. Without the leaven of so much as a prickle of carbonic gas, the wine was positively pyrrhic in its hesitant pace, indeed four steps to the right and two to the left going all the way down.

14

DIAMONDS IN THE ROUGH

For some years until it closed I was a big-ticket customer at Para Liquors in the Astoria section of Queens, New York. Named for its owner, Mr. Paralikas, Para Liquors catered to the Greek community and carried a wide selection of Greek wines. I would show up from Virginia about every four months and haul back cases of assorted Greek wines I could not find anywhere closer to home. There were always new wines, too, since the Greek importers based in Queens tended to shift their allegiances among homeland wine producers with the frequency of the ancient Greek city-states switching political alliances. But even so, my greatest find at Para came in the unlikely form of Johnny Ternas, a gregarious sales clerk there. Johnny would spot me as soon as I entered, and knowing a serious buyer on sight he would drop whatever he was doing and attend to me immediately. He could never do enough to advise me, like the time he unscrewed the cap from a bottle of Cyprus Muscat and urged me with a confident "Smell that!" as he thrust the mouth of the bottle under my nose. I hardly had time for a deep inhalation before Johnny recapped the bottle and stuck it in my shopping cart without comment from me.

Mainland Greece

But it was also Johnny who attacked me with the same element of surprise on another occasion and put me onto the scent of Siatista. My mouth surely must have dropped open the first time he mentioned the place. I flipped fruitlessly through the mental list of place-names I had accumulated from contemporary wine literature. Johnny might just as well have said Timbuktu. I was relieved to find out that his knowledge did not stem from rigorous connoisseurship, but from chance parentage. Johnny's parents were from western Macedonia, and his mother's hometown was Siatista. His praise for the place's sweet *liasto* wine was lavish and would have left me thinking that the 20-year-old kind in particular occupies a seat among the world's consummate wine experiences – had I been inclined to take the word of anyone as sanguine as Johnny was about screw-top wine bottles.

Being more a believer in the printed than the spoken word, I stopped off at the Library of Congress in Washington, D.C., to check out Johnny's implausible story even before I got home to Virginia to unload my wines. I was amazed to find him borne out in the several exhaustive bibles about the Balkan Peninsula written by early 19th century European visitors. The Frenchman Ami Boué (*La Turquie d'Europe*, 1840) listed Siatista first in naming several places he thought deserved special mention for their wines; and the Englishman William Leake (*Travels in Northern Greece*, 1835) mentioned Siatista's sweet wine by name (*lioumenon*). But most of all it was Leake's relation of the demise of a Siatistan winebibber that caught my attention:

> ... [at Siatista] the people [are] more curious in their tables than any I have met with in Greece. This, as the stipendiary physician of the place observes to me, is almost the only source of disease, so healthy is the air and situation. But they drink he remarks, rather too much of their own good wine, of which one of his patients is an example, who is now dying of the effects of a fall from his horse, after an indulgence of that kind.

Siatista immediately became a must destination, and on my next visit to Para I pumped Johnny for more information. Even more pleased about having sold me on the out-of-reach *liasto* than on the Muscat at hand, he heartily recommended that I carry through on my plan to visit the town, and referred me to his Aunt Marigo there.

Siatista must have been the sort of place that gave rise to the Greek adage, 'a village that appears needs no guide.' The town was nowhere in sight, and without road signs to point the way I almost despaired of finding it. While my map showed it lying between Grevena and Kozani, once I was actually on the ground the overgrown fields and nearly barren mountain slopes along the road gave me no clue as to where an inhabited place might be. But my book learning by that time had informed me that Siatista is an old center of the Macedonian fur trade, and I got the 'guide' I needed when in the middle of nowhere I came across the Macedonian equivalent of a factory outlet store for furs. I took the next turn off the main road and passed first through a cleft in the mountains and then through the remnants of what once must have been the town gateway. At the top of the road indeed stood Siatista.

Finding Johnny's Aunt Marigo was a snap. The first person I encountered knew her and pointed out her home. It was not at all far off and sat behind a little portal and courtyard. But Siatista is not the Greece of stucco-and-whitewash Aegean cubes. Aunt Marigo's home was a substantial one constructed for weather in which jackets are not put away until June and grapes are not harvested until well into October. My knock on the door produced Aunt Marigo herself, who struck me as a complete anachronism. Dressed in black workaday clothing that had a regional cut to it, she spoke in such strongly dialectical Greek that my ears had all they could do to follow her syllables. But I did understand that she was in the middle of cheese-making. This seemed both fitting and promising. It was fitting because the town's name may be an amalgam of the names Shatir ('Tent'), given to an early part of the settlement by Vlach shepherds, and Tiritza ('Cheese-burg'), given to a later part by a Greek Orthodox metropolitan; and promising because this was obviously a household that satisfied its own tastes.

Greek Salad

Aunt Marigo quickly handed me over to her son, Johnny's cousin, and went back to her curds and whey. Apparently on Johnny's past inculcation of English, the cousin introduced himself as 'Dzordz' (George). He did not look at all like Johnny, but his resemblance in manner was uncanny. Just like his American cousin, Dzordz came at me with a helpful familiarity that transcended the Greeks' usual probing hospitality, in slightly quirky ways. He immediately took me on a no-rooms-barred inspection tour of the premises, and as if saving the best for last we finished off at the bathroom, whose elaborate plumbing Dzordz obviously expected me to find endlessly fascinating.

I thought hydraulics might be his line, but when I asked him about his work he replied that it is furs. Every fall he would fill up his car with furs and head up through Yugoslavia to Hungary, Czechoslovakia and Poland to sell them off. In short order, I found myself outside with Dzordz, the two of us peering into the engine of his Orient Express jalopy. Of course that was not the end of it, because we also had to cram into the car and take the tour of Siatista, with a stop now and then so that Dzordz could introduce "a friend of Dzonni."

Faded signs of one-time wealth were apparent everywhere along our route. The town had prospered handsomely from the fur trade with central Europe during Ottoman times and even became an intellectual center (the first Greek newspaper – 'Newspaper' – was published in Siatista in 1790). The same routes known to Dzordz had been plied by the Macedonians for generations on end going back to antiquity and Hellenic commercial interest in amber from the Baltic area. In the late Middle Ages the Greeks were so active in commerce in Poland that by 1700 they had taken over the trade of Hungary's Tokay wine. Most of these Greeks were from Macedonia, and I found Siatista impressive enough to make me think that a few of those traders must have been Siatistans. While on this train of thought I also mused that I might even have an ancestral share in this Macedonian connection because Greeks were the first owners of a village just two miles down the road from an ancestral hamlet of mine in northern Hungary in the 13th century. Anyway, not even communism had managed to shut down the ancient routes, albeit Dzordz's car showed every bit of injury that communist Balkan roadways could inflict on democratic Greek vehicles.

When Dzordz and I finally returned to the starting gate we went directly to the only space in the house that we had not previously viewed, the wine cellar. From my readings of the 19th century European travelers I had somewhat grandiose expectations about Siatista's cellars. Siatistan traders in the old days had been as far as Germany, and along with the printing press had brought back knowledge of the latest cellar techniques, which they lost no time in putting to use in their homes. Leake mentioned that all the larger houses in the town had cellars beneath them, with a fastidious arrangement of wine butts "as in civilized Europe." However, the cellar Dzordz took me into was only on the ground floor, off from the dining room. We found Aunt Marigo there – making the cheese of course. Behind her were three oak barrels of enormous size, relics of the infinitely better days for Siatistan wine growers before the phylloxera pest decimated the town's vineyards in the early part of the 20th century.

I expected Dzordz to draw wine from one of the barrels but instead he reached down to a cubby-hole and pulled out a home-corked bottle. Back in the dining room he uncorked it and poured us a bit of its incipiently brownish red contents into two tumblers. The wine was a 15-year-old dry one in a condition that tweaks the nose of cosmopolitan professionals of the Greek wine industry who come down hard on their compatriots in technologically stranded wine places like Siatista for having no appreciation of freshness in wine. Certainly it seemed that Dzordz appreciated age on wine virtually for its own sake.

Dzordz was in no hurry to move on to the sweet *liasto* wine he knew Johnny had sent me for. Instead he spoke at some length about his travels in central Europe and his ways of doing business there while circumventing communist red-tape. He was delighted that I could scribble for him in Greek transliteration some Berlitz and non-Berlitz Hungarian phrases he thought would be helpful on his forays into Budapest peddling furs. But when I brought him back to wine and *liasto* he described Siatistan cellar practices in more detail than he had the bathroom plumbing. My note-taking could not keep up with him. Fortunately I had read about some of it in the old books at the Library of Congress.

Liasto wine is found widely in Greece. It literally means 'sunned' and refers to the fact that the grapes are harvested and then dried a bit to increase sugar content before the wine making begins. An important local deviation mentioned by Dzordz was that the grape-must for Siatista's *liasto* is separated from the grape-skins by filtering through a mesh of clean goat's wool. This procedure might shed some light on the question of the techniques the ancient Greeks had for filtering wine. Plutarch recorded a debate on filtration in which the defender of the practice argued that "those who draw off the impurities and unpalatable elements are simply tending and cleaning" the wine. Although the Siatistans in effect moved filtering several steps forward to must-making, they too had a cleansing purpose in mind with their goat's wool technique. But such is the isolation of the place today that no enologists will be traipsing off to Siatista anytime soon to look into the matter further.

The household's *liasto* was resting in a small chestnut cask in the cellar. As soon as Aunt Marigo saw Dzordz come to draw some she abandoned the cheese and rushed out of the cellar and into the dining

Greek Salad

room to replace our tumblers with stemware Dzordz had brought back from Poland or Czechoslovakia or Hungary. Dzordz then poured the amberish liquid. Its bouquet was possessed of some singular aromatic nuances and was also distinguished by an aromatic lightness that called to mind something that Theophrastus (*Concerning Odours*) suggested about a swift but soft penetration of the nasal passages up to what might be thought of as the 'upper register' of smell sensors. While I must prudently remain dubious about the role of the goat's wool in all this, there is no doubt that Siatista was the best thing Johnny Ternas ever pushed under my nose.

15

EPISTLES TO THE MACEDONIANS

Naoussa, Macedonia
May 23, 1983
3 a.m.

Dear Mom and Dad,

I feel like Aunt Fran, writing a letter at such an early hour. But I've lost the fight against the sorriest excuse for a bed I ever paid drachmas to sleep on. The mattress is all of two inches thick and is laid over a plywood board nearly an inch thick. It's hard to believe this hotel is classed in the 'C' category. I usually stay in C's and have never run into anything like this before. I guess so few tourists come to Naoussa that the Greek hoteliers' association doesn't bother to send out its bed-testers. But don't imagine I'm in the boonies. Naoussa is most definitely a town, an industrialized one in fact.

Speaking of Aunt Fran, she's had me looking for a certain kind of metal bracelet my last three trips to Greece. This time she even sent me a sketch: two inches wide and gold-colored, with a floral pattern. Maybe there's a chance of finding something like it here in Macedonia. There seems to be a whole crafts industry based on replicas of artifacts from the time of Alexander the Great. Most of it is heavy and imposing stuff like Aunt Fran goes for. I may not find what she wants here in Naoussa, but maybe I can when I get to Salonika (the main city of Macedonia, about 30 miles east of here). I sure don't want to be sent on a wild goose chase again on my next visit.

Yesterday I was lucky in getting around town. I ran out of note-pads late in the afternoon, bought one at a kiosk, sat down on a bench to scribble, and got into a conversation with an already seated shopkeeper who had closed up for the afternoon siesta. As you might expect in a small town, he 'knows everyone' in Naoussa. He took me to meet the several locals who are making and bottling wine on a small scale. We went into the vineyards below town to chase down one of them, to the apartment of another, and to the shop of a third. Without the shopkeeper I could have wasted the whole time trying to find any one of them, and probably without success. He stayed with me until well into the evening. I wonder whether he ever even bothered to go back to his shop. It just shows how desperate for strangers the Naoussans must be. Anyway, too bad I didn't think to ask him about bracelets.

*   *   *

Mainland Greece

Naoussa, Macedonia
May 23, 1983
7 a.m.

Dear Kevin,

I'm writing to you from a bench in the park in front of the hotel where I'm putting up (with a lot). I'm facing more or less east and getting the sunrise, but it's not getting in my eyes enough as yet to thwart my writing. Orchards and vineyards are spread out before me 'as far as the eye can see.' All I need is a prayer rug.

I'm sure you'll recognize Naoussa's name. We drank a bottle of wine from here not long ago. You were fascinated by the old Greek printing on the label, remember? Or else, maybe you remember discoursing on Aristotelian metaphysics by the time the wine was gone. I think you were saying something about whether wine exists in the abstract as 'wine-ness.' There are nooks in Attica where I could meditate on that, but not here in Macedonia. I suspect it's the difference in light and vegetation. This is Zorba's neck of the woods, you may recall. Just imagine Zorba's response if Aristotle asked him to ponder 'flesh' apart from "the female sex, in person"!

'Wine-ness' or not, yesterday I tasted two superb wines. One came from the rolling Strandza area below town, and the other from the upland area of Pola Nera.

Greek Salad

The names don't mean anything now, but in fifty years who knows? And you might start practicing the name of the local grape, xynomavro – you won't sound any worse than my mother pronouncing pinot noir. Anyhow, I would like to have heard your descriptive commentary on the wines. I could almost hear you splitting the hairs. Don't take that as criticism of your penchant for detail. I'm just pointing out that Naoussa has a full head of vinous hair for wine buffs to untangle.

The food has been good, if occasionally somewhat eccentric even by Balkan standards. How does a dish of beans stewed with prunes sound? (On second thought, I retract the question – nobody should know how it sounds.) A shopkeeper I met yesterday told me Naoussa used to be famous for its savory pitas (pies) and carried on an export trade in them. Wine trade, I can feature. But pies?! They did have camels in Macedonia a couple centuries ago when caravans were going north into central Europe, but even so, how many pies to a hump?

* * *

Mainland Greece

Naoussa, Macedonia
May 23, 1983
8 a.m.

Dear Gary,

I'm up near the northern reaches of Greece. This is not the Greece we learned about from Dr. Quest. I mean, this is 'dark' and mystical Greece, not the Greece of rational thought. The ancient Greeks of our acquaintance had qualms about the Macedonians as Hellenes (not as to descent and dialect, but Culture), and Alexander himself once asked two guests from the Hellenic south whether they did not feel like demigods among savages.

The hotel where I'm staying offers neither bed nor breakfast (I'll explain that when I see you), so I am presently sitting in the main square of Naoussa having a bucolic picnic breakfast of cheese-and-leek pita (pie) and milk, which I picked up in a sort of dairy carry-out shop. To tell you the truth, though, I'm just as glad the hotel doesn't offer breakfast, because it's C class and in Greece that usually means stale manufactured biscuits and thin industrial marmalade. You'd think some repatriated Greeks who worked for decades in American diners would start serving real breakfasts. But it hasn't happened yet, and it wouldn't work in Naoussa in any case since tourists don't come here, except for this wine-crazed one.

Greek Salad

I hope the pita-and-milk combination doesn't sound too barbaric to you. Yes, I'm sure the pita would taste better with wine, but wine belongs to the night, and nowhere more so than here in Macedonia. Besides, this particular pita is nothing to write home about. I can do better myself on a good day (I'll have to make my sautéed cabbage and calamata olive pita for our next wine tasting – with Naoussan wines, of course).

I'm planning to visit the two major wineries here today. I devoted yesterday to the minor producers (I'm not calling their wines minor). Most places in Greece don't have so many commercial wine producers as yet. It's odd how the tables have turned and left the Macedonians ahead of the other Greeks in that great symbol of civilization – wine. Yesterday one of the producers told me he "always wanted to produce a château wine." Where does a Macedonian get off thinking like that?! Of course, though, as a former student of Dr. Quest I do not think 'château wine' in itself says much about the state of civilization. As a matter of fact, my back is telling me mattresses say much more about it, but that's part of my hotel story.

* * *

Mainland Greece

Naoussa, Macedonia
May 23, 1983
2 p.m.

Dear Jon,

Well of course I had to write you from Macedonia, budding 'old Balkan hand' that you are. If you get out your maps you'll see I'm smack in the middle of what sometimes used to be called 'Aegean Macedonia,' or the southernmost chunk of what the Ottoman Turks called Macedonia. The place-names might vary depending on the age of the map. Most places had alternative names in Greek and Turkish or Bulgarian (also known as Slavo-Macedonian hereabouts). Naoussa, for instance, was also known as Negush. But my favorite in that way is the superb nearby wine village of Pola Nera, which also had the name Fetishcha. I don't know whether the origin is Turkish, Slavic or Vlach, but a wine fetishist has to appreciate the irony of it.

By the way, the Greek view is that the term 'Macedonian' is an historical one associated specifically with a people of Hellenic culture and may not be used by groups that arrived later no matter how long they have lived on any territory that at any time has been known as Macedonia. Maybe it's like saying that we could take up residence in Florida but never call ourselves Seminoles. The hitch in my analogy is that there certainly was plenty of inter-ethnic breeding in Macedonia in the past since the Christians were all

Greek Salad

Orthodox and bilingualism was common. (Hmm, a lot of unusually tall and fair Greeks up here.)

Today I was in the village of Stenimachos, below Naoussa, to visit a large modern winery. The village is populated by Greek refugees who came from a town of that name (now called Assenovgrad) in Bulgaria as part of a population exchange in the 1920s. They were expert vine-dressers in Bulgaria, which explains why they ended up at Naoussa. The winery displays an old still for making 'raki' (Balkan schnapps), which the refugees brought with them. It has Bulgarian writing on it and I'm a little surprised that Greeks would prize it. Maybe their subliminal stress is on the negative (as in pogrom), for the sake of keeping an ethnic wound open.

I picked up some background about this part of Macedonia from an old man I met through Irena, 'Uncle Chris.' He was originally from the next town north of here, Edessa, and spoke several of the languages that were typical of the region in his youth. He left Greece because of a repressive regime in the 1930s and has resided in Sofia ever since (the poor fellow had no inkling of the repression that was headed for Bulgaria). In any case, Uncle Chris was a font of information on life here before the Balkan Wars. He also remembered all the outstanding Macedonian wine villages of yesteryear. He once sent me a folk 'recipe' (as he called it) for wine, but I am not sure whether it is Greek or Slav or just generic Macedonian. It starts off, "Harvest your worst grapes and sell them to Turks to make raki…" That might explain why an old Naoussan I met last evening insisted that Naoussan wine was better in the old days!

*   *   *

Naoussa, Macedonia
May 23, 1983
3:00 p.m.

Dear Marie,

I've just finished lunch in a taverna here in Naoussa, a town about an hour west of Salonika. It was a late lunch even by Greek schedules. Actually, I was lucky to get any at all. I got here about half an hour ago, and the woman running the place was putting the food away and getting ready to close for the afternoon. Fortunately, she still had some of the midday special sitting out. It's a kind of beef ragoût called 'tas-kebab.'

The names of many of the local dishes, like tas kebab, sound Turkish – and the Greeks will jump down your throat if you mention it. They say the Turks gave Turkish names to foods that were already being made here. They might have a point in some cases. After all, the Greeks were certainly making stews like tas-kebab when kebab meant nothing more to the Turks than charred meat on a stick.

There's plenty of variety. Macedonia grows just about everything you could want. Well, there's no radicchio yet, nor most of those other chi-chi ingredients they highlight in your cuisine magazines. But still, you can eat better than well if you set your nose to it and keep your eyes open. Like, for instance, the fish soup in Salonika at a restaurant bearing Naoussa's name makes me think of that 5-star compliment you sometimes pay to wines – "the best thing I ever put in my mouth" (you know I wouldn't say that about a fish soup with tomato).

I'm sitting here passing time with a whole bottle of wine all to myself. You'd think in an old wine town like Naoussa there'd be a home-made local wine on tap so customers could order just a glass. But all that's available in this place are regular-size bottles of commercially made stuff. I haven't progressed very far with this bottle, but its price is such that I don't mind how much of it I'm going to leave behind. I'm sure you couldn't afford to think like that when you were in Burgundy. And take my word for it, this wine is hardly behind most Burgundy. But the label trails by a few lengths.

That reminds me of something a local enologist told me this morning (I'm copying from my note-pad, in the original English of the statement): "We

Mainland Greece

(Greeks) never have a good entrance, but inside you can find good things." That goes for this taverna too. Hotels are another story.

*   *   *

Naoussa, Macedonia,
6:00 p.m.
May 23, 1983

Dear Marshall,

Greetings from Macedonia! I'm sorry I don't have your photography skills. My photos are not going to do the region justice.

How are things back at Agriculture? Much as I hate to admit it, USDA flashes through my mind from time to time. But I can hardly help it since this area is wonderfully suited to various branches of farming. (Tell Reed I said central Macedonia is the Po Valley of Greece. Maybe he'll send me back on a field trip sometime.) Oriental tobacco is the really big cash crop in much of Macedonia, including the parts in neighboring Yugoslavia and Bulgaria, but around Naoussa it doesn't amount to a cigarette butt. Wineries, canneries and spinning mills are what they've got here, and you know which I came for.

Greek Salad

Tomorrow I'll be going to Salonika. Tell Reed I'll be meeting with a professor from the university to talk about livestock. It's amazing how pork production and consumption have soared in Greece in recent years. The industry has wheedled a lot of crypto-support from the government, which is why pork is just about the only kind of souvlaki you find these days. My favorite promotional measure is the designation of 'pork days' in restaurants. Apparently both the restaurants and the customers get a price break. Anyway, I know a taverna in Salonika that features some unusual pork dishes along with outstanding rustic bread. But pardon me for yapping at <u>you</u> about pork!

Salonika and pork – now there's an historical irony. Salonika was over one-third Jewish (Sephardic, not Ashkenazi) during Turkish times and right through World War I. In fact, because Turks and Slavs as well as Greeks lived there, the Jews were usually a plurality of the population. Apparently the city practically used to shut down on Fridays because there was hardly any occupation in which Jews were not critical to the labor force, whether 'blue turban' or 'white turban.' And now – pork days!

Anyhow, Salonika is the jewel of Macedonia as far as I'm concerned. No wonder the Yugoslavs and Bulgarians have drooled over possessing it. I'm sure you'd find it photogenic. I especially like sitting at cafés along the seaside promenade close to the 15th century White Tower (the city emblem) around sunset.

Mainland Greece

At home at that time of day I'd be commuting, just when I need to 'unjangle' my nerves. I've never been in a big city and felt the transition from day to evening go so smoothly as in Salonika. I just sit and watch the sea and collect my thoughts. And by the way, I know a café where you could capture a great photo of the White Tower upside down through a glass of ouzo.

*   *   *

Naoussa, Macedonia
May 23, 1983
8:30 p.m.

Dear Aunt Fran and Uncle Gene,

I'm writing from the austere armchair in my hotel room. But the chair beats the bed. I have no mattress to speak of and I'm trying to devise a sleeping strategy for tonight. Alexander the Great supposedly slept like a log with a dagger and a copy of the Iliad under his pillow, but obviously he was of sterner – or else thicker – stuff (with the Macedonians one can't always be sure which). I would prefer the sort of travelers' inn they would have had here back in Turkish times, where they just gave you a pile of straw to lay on. But this is the only 'barn' in town at the present time.

Greek Salad

I've never been in a Greek town Naoussa's size before and not seen any other tourists. It's ironic that there was a time when virtually any European who came to Macedonia visited Naoussa, whereas now practically none of the millions who deluge Greece get here. Well, Naoussa has neither beaches nor antiquities, and who comes to Greece for anything else? Actually, I think Naoussa could someday hold its own, touristically speaking, and attract people besides the odd few like me who come because of its wine reputation. Some of the older homes (most of which were built by wealthy wine merchants two centuries ago) could be a draw. But the old part of town needs sprucing up. And the Naoussans are going to have to start offering mattresses as well.

Tomorrow I'm off to Salonika, the chief city of northern Greece. It's Athens' modern rival. Generally, I prefer Salonika to Athens because it's less crowded and the air is cleaner. I'm sure the two of you would too because there's something more 'continental' about Salonika despite the ouzo and baklava (I even know a bakery that does a great Macedonian take on apple pie). And Uncle Gene wouldn't be beset at every turn by "the old stones" that put him off about Athens. Maybe you could visit in connection with his tobacco industry dealings since plenty of tobacco gets shipped from Salonika. I can assure you that Salonika beats Richmond as a destination.

Mainland Greece

Salonika is good for shopping too, and by the way, Aunt Fran, I'm not having any luck finding that bracelet for you. I have seen metal bracelets, and some had ancient motifs, like the 16-point Macedonian star, but nothing floral like you want (I suppose the ancient Macedonians were too martial to have been motivated by 'flower power'). But you might drive into Astoria and ask about it in some of the Greek import stores I showed you. Or, since Cousin Gene does art work in metal, do you suppose he would be willing to hammer one out for you? I'll be glad to send him the design you sent me.

*   *   *   *   *

16

PEREGRINATIONS ON A GRECIAN CUP

It's an unremarkable cup, short and plain, just a two-tone ceramic cup, unglazed from the bottom to around midway up, and then glazed from the finger ring to the lip and on down inside, with the Greek words 'Rapsani Wine Festival' painted in a whitewash on the glazed portion. But homely as it is, it's the only *real* keepsake I have from Greece – something left over from an actual incident in my travels there, not just the incidental purchase of a souvenir.

Even better, nothing in my possession beats this cup for mulling over wine and Greece and the ancients. Even empty, I find it brimming with Dionysian lore and mystery – bulls, satyrs, snakes, nymphs, baskets, beehives, ecstasy, orgasm, death, rebirth. My mind careens down the subconscious labyrinths of the wine-god.

But, first things first. Rapsani? A village in Thessaly, on the flank of Mount Kissavos, the ancient Ossa. Rapsani wine?! Hardly known outside Greece and at its source a proof that the Greeks have never been able or willing to separate wine from the passions.

There was a time when I held Rapsani's red wine in great esteem because the only one available in bottle

168

(and labeled simply *Rapsani*) was like no other wine I knew, not in color, not in feel, and maybe most of all not in mood effect. At home once when there was a physical threat to my motley wine stash and I removed a case of my most valuable wines – price unconsidered – to a safer place, I put my only remaining bottle of *Rapsani* in it along with some touted and far more expensive companions. Having paid homage at such a remove from Ossa, I of course wanted to do so on the spot when I got the chance.

The chance came one late September day while heading south on the National Road from dairy meetings in Macedonia to pork meetings in the Peloponnesos. I suggested to my Greek guide, Nick, from the U.S. Embassy in Athens, that we stop off at Rapsani. Nick could not have cared less about the wine of Rapsani, but he liked to keep track of his land travels in Greece by coloring over on a wall map in his office the roads he had traversed, and he was game for chalking up the squiggle between the National Road and Rapsani, which he had not driven before.

We left pavement for macadam just beyond the Vale of Tempe and slowly wound our way up for several miles into the foothills of Ossa. Nick and I had the road to ourselves, as though nobody knew or cared about Rapsani wine. But the village thought it had an audience, because preparations were being completed for the first annual Rapsani wine festival, to be held that weekend, in late September. Tables and chairs covered the *plateia*, and barrels plastered with the *Rapsani* label so familiar to me were in place in the center of the space. Nick, a veteran of many official U.S. Department of Agriculture rural excursions, soon rounded up several village elders qualified to talk about growing, harvesting and producing Rapsani wine, and we all settled in for a powwow at a table beside a tree on the *plateia*.

Wine was offered and I accepted, while Nick demurred and opted instead for the later-day Greek sacrament of coffee and a cigarette. I was brought an earthen mug filled at the barrels, and I found the wine even more 'rough and tumble' than I remembered my accustomed *Rapsani* wine to be. An official from the local wine cooperative that produced it explained that this wine was still two years away from bottling. But I had hardly touched that wine when our conversation turned to peasant wine making habits and a mug of a different wine was brought to me from a nearby *taverna*. This second wine was produced from grapes that had hung longer on the vine, and had fermented a longer time on the skins than the first wine. It was the tougher and headier of the two.

I stuck with the peasant wine, if only out of curiosity about 'the real stuff' of Rapsani. But I did not drink much at all, did not even empty the l-cup measure mug during the half-hour or so that we continued to chat; and up in that clear and invigorating mountain atmosphere the wine seemed to have no effect on me whatsoever. But as soon as Nick and I descended from Rapsani and bottomed out at the Thessalian plain, the home-made vintage of Rapsani rained down on my head like a slide of ceramic tiles from the village's rooftops. I was woozy. I thought I must have found Homer's otherwise unspecified *theion poton* – 'divine drink.' For surely the wine that was bringing me down had been meant for the Olympians, not for ordinary mortals like me.

*

It seemed fitting that Ossa is just one mountain mass over from Mount Olympus, the lair of those spirited and treacherous Greek gods, and the cradle as well of that most carousing of mortal Greeks, Alexis Zorbas. Neither the Olympians nor Zorba would take solace in our Elegant Wine. The Rapsani wine I drank on the *plateia* was a rebuke to our notion that a vinous paragon needs to be an unrelieved experience in such attributes as 'perfect balance' and 'silky smoothness.' Rapsani *brousko* instead had teeth and raw nerve, and challenged the wine lover to show some of Zorba's gumption: "The god-devil sends you this choice morsel. You've got teeth. All right, get'em into it…Now's the time you're going to save or lose your soul."

Save my soul indeed. That peasant wine of Rapsani was a hard-core *brousko*. Wine of its kind must have been made in Greece at a very early date. Even

Greek Salad

the Greek name for the grapevine, *ampelos*, might be a testament to *brousko*'s age. In ancient Greek mythology, Ampelos was a beautiful satyr possessed of spirit and vigor, who was dearly loved by Dionysus himself. Ampelos was especially fond of riding a certain very wild bull, and one day was thrown and killed by it. Dionysus intervened before Ampelos could reach the underworld and asked Zeus to transform the satyr into a plant. Zeus obliged his son by fashioning the grapevine as the embodiment of Ampelos and his fate.

Brousko's name, however, is Italian, not Greek. The Greeks adopted the Italian for 'rough' and 'sharp' wine during the late Middle Ages, when they came under widespread Venetian influence. Presumably they liked the onomatopoeic skid to *brrruuusco*, which so well suits this brisk, brusque and bruising wine. But during antiquity the Greeks described wine of *brousko* type by their own word *afstiros*, or 'austere,' which Plato specified as a rough sort of drying sensation. This sensation in wine characteristically occurred in combination with certain others: Eparhides described the Pramnian wine of Ikaria as "neither sweet, nor fat, but *afstiros*, hard, and of extraordinary strength." His formulation is remarkably close to a Greek encyclopedia definition of *brousko* two millennia later: "astringent, rough, and sometimes tart wine, in which the taste of alcohol and acid is stronger than that of sugar."

Mainland Greece

Wetness is a tenuous sensation in any *brousko* up to scratch. It is really a wonder that anyone manages to eke refreshment out of such wine. The 'quench' of a *brousko* is almost a contradiction in terms, and is peculiar in not removing all memory of the condition that originally provoked the thirst. Quite the opposite, *brousko*, by its raspy play in the mouth, reminds us of our thirst even while refreshment, such as it might be, is underway. This reminder gives rise to a visceral reaction whose appeal to the Greeks perhaps is best appreciated through a sympathy for the staccato laments of the old-style *bouzouki* songs known as *rebetika*, the Greek 'blues.' In one such song, a woman invites a soldier: "Forget the barracks and sentry-boxes, and drink from the *brousko* of our hearts." The songs are inspired by the yearning that the Greeks call *kaïmos* (literally 'burning'), which is always something to be quelled rather than extinguished, since no Greek would want to live without it.

*

My cup had been used only that one time in Rapsani. At home it sat for years on tables and shelves collecting dust and serving as a convenient receptacle for stray coins and paper clips. But I brought the cup out of retirement recently for one more use, to once again stain its inside with its native vintage, a bottle of *Kentavros* from the 1991 vintage. It had been given to me in 1994 by its producer, and my friend in wine, Kosta Mitrakos, who had begun bottling his Rapsani wine several years after my visit to the village. But Kosta had died suddenly in 1996 and my bottle of his 1991 would be the last of his wine that I would taste.

There would be *kaïmos* enough for me in Kosta's *Kentavros* no matter its condition. But despite a decade in bottle, the wine had not mellowed, had not lost its 'teeth.' Kosta was always trying to 'perfect' his wine, but I don't think he ever aimed to 'tame' it; otherwise he would not have named it *Kentavros* – Centaur.

Staring into my cup of Kosta's wine, I found myself recollecting my long-ago morning in Rapsani's school of hard knocks and drifting off to thoughts of Dionysus, *brousko*, treachery, snakes, and also, the *syrtos* – the 'dragging' dance of antiquity. This was because of a forgotten detail of my visit, when one of the villagers who sat with us at the table on the *plateia* said that Nick and I ought to stay the night because there would be plenty of *brousko* and music and dancing – "a *glendi*." 'Party' might be a translation for it, but a true Grecian *glendi* has all the marks of descending from the bacchanalia of antiquity. "Wine and dancing go together," the man had added, and he might just as well have said that the Greeks throughout history have never expected to drink wine and *not* dance. Some things after all are as heady as *brousko*:

"We must be especially wary of these pleasures:
[Music and dance] are extremely powerful because

they do not, like those of taste and touch and smell have their only effect in the irrational and 'natural' part of our mind, but lay hold of our faculty of judgement and prudence."

(Lamprias, in Plutarch's *Table-talk*)

And surely the dance that was going to dominate the *glendi* would be the *syrtos*. Like *brousko*, the *syrtos* is another anachronism recalling Dionysian times.

Rapsani is a mountain village and ancient Greek myth placed the original worship of Dionysus in mountain caves where bees had their hives. Honey was associated with the wine-god because its sweetness can be transformed into vinousness by fermentation. But the caves were also inhabited by snakes, and this set the ancient erotic imagination aflame in trying to reckon the nature of Dionysus. To us it is manifest mostly in the ancient artwork depicting ichthyphallic satyrs working the vintage. But it all owed originally to using the mountain cave snakes in the earliest Dionysian rituals. To celebrate the god's biennial cycle of birth, death and resurrection – in tandem with the cycle of the grapevine – a snake was cut into seven pieces and carried ceremonially in a covered basket by women devotees to symbolize the dismemberment and restoration of Bacchus. The rise-fall-and-rise-again metaphor imparted phallic connotations to the wine-god. It was death and resurrection seen metaphysically as an erotic transcendence.

Greek Salad

But the snakes are also why the winding labyrinth was embraced as the self-chosen, divine pattern of the wine-god. Recalling this epoch, the classicist Carl Kerényi saw in the steps and serpentine progression of the still popular *syrtos* dance the master-key to the Classical meander pattern. Well, the Greeks do hark back to the Dionysian snakes when they say that something has "broken in 42 pieces," which is 7 times 6, from the seven snake pieces multiplied by the six slices needed to make them.

Akh! Kaïmos! How I wished now, as I drank deeply from the *Kentavros* in my cup, that I had let Nick go on without me that day in Rapsani twenty years ago and had stayed to dance the *syrtos* and quaff *brousko* for as long as the *glendi* went on. Just to resurrect Dionysus for a spell.

17

GREASY SPOON

The Greek diet may not have changed fundamentally since the days when Hippocrates wrote *Regimen*. But in the early 1980s the northern European meat-and-potatoes regime was giving The Father of Medicine a run for the money on his home turf. One sign of the changing times was increasing demand for cold cuts and canned luncheon meat, which was putting Greek pigs on the chopping block at a hot pace. To check on the latest developments on that front for USDA, I arranged a couple of meetings along my route south from Salonika to Athens one spring day. The morning was spent deep in soybean meal at a live-stock-feed plant near Katerini in southern coastal Macedonia. For the afternoon I had an appointment at a pork-processing plant near the Thessalian capital of Larissa to have a look at the tragic side of livestock rations. I decided to brighten my day with an impromptu stop in between at the wine cooperative of Tyrnavos on the lowlands of Thessaly, the granary of ancient Greece and still known more for its wheat than its wine.

The Tyrnavos wines may only have been plain in flavor but they induced appetite nonetheless. I would need to eat something before the inevitable canned ham samples were offered at my next appointment.

Greek Salad

Not being acquainted with Larissa, I asked the winery manager as I was leaving whether he could recommend a place to eat. He immediately answered that he was sure I would like "Godis" – or at least that was how I heard and jotted down the name he gave me. I thought Godis must be either the owner's somewhat peculiar surname, or else the name of a minor figure in Greek mythology that I had forgotten about. The decisive recommendation was encouraging in any case because I presumed I was being sent to a kitchen known for its local specialties. I could have slapped my forehead when Godis turned out to be the Larissa branch of the Goody's chain of fast-food hamburger houses, which unbeknownst to me had begun its own Trojan horse invasion of the age-old Greek diet. Even plain wine stimulates higher expectations for lunch.

I was profoundly dismayed by the winery boss's presumption that I would prefer Goody's to any other commercial kitchen he knew in Larissa. The Greeks apparently had been cowed into suet by decades of listening to visiting Anglo-Saxons moan and drone about olive oil. Just shortly before my trip to Greece a British agricultural economist visiting my work group in Washington declared with arrestingly candid subjectivity that surplus Mediterranean olive oil could never be drained into Britain at any price because the taste for it simply would never be acquired by a significant number of Brits. This was accompanied by vocal tones and facial contortions conveying disgust at the very thought of the gunk. But I had a taste for olive oil ever since I first met it tongue on. In Greece I seek out back-street olive oil shrines where the glistening pans of food illuminate otherwise dingy interiors. Just a gander at the pans informs me whether the medium is understood by the practitioner. Olive oil after all is slippery business and not just anyone will do.

I beat a hasty retreat from Goody's and a few blocks away found a *taverna* where several generously lacquered specials were on view. Mostly they were *ladera* dishes. The name denotes 'oiled ones' and to an English-accustomed ear it sounds enough like 'lathered' to grease the funny bone with the accurate degree of exuberance it suggests. The theory behind the *ladera* is that they should cook until the watery part of the juices issuing from the vegetables, as well as any other liquid ingredients that might be included, has evaporated, so that the food is left standing, not to say sliding, on its oil. The *ladera* are not, however, to be glossed over. One Greek cookbook authoress called them "the basis of our subsistence." In Greece, where the olive tree has always been profuse, the olive's ooze naturally became for poor people a major source of calories, not just a cooking medium.

Two workmen seated in the Larissa *taverna* were both eating gleaming green okra as a main course. I was sorely tempted to follow suit, but a plateful of okra and olive oil can take an out-of-practice intestinal track by surprise. I decided that resisting sore temptation would be the better part of valor – or at least eas-

Greek Salad

ier to live with on the road than the soreness I could be in for if I did not resist. I responded instead to the wild call of a viscous and resplendent *mousaka*.

To my way of thinking a proper *mousaka* is an olive oil dish par excellence, though for strict constructionists it does not belong to the genus *ladera*. In fact its classification is a bit of a head-scratcher and probably depends mostly on how one can best slice it. *Mousaka* certainly cannot lay with the *en croûte* delicacies; but on the other hand it does not sink with the fluid casseroles, either. Sometimes it seems to slide in between the *terrines* and *pâtés*: it leans toward *terrines* if it is of the high-built kind and served at Aegean room temperature when several days old; and toward *pâtés* if it is also crusty and baked with a lining of eggplant skins. However, the rarer low-built *mousaka*, with its slim strata, cuts nicely on the bias and, if highly flavored with sweet spices, can for all the world seem a soft, non-stick *baklava*.

Mousaka has never been a fixed edifice. It has a checkered past, diffuse geographical tendrils and a plethora of variations on the general theme. To slosh under the umbrella of *mousaka* a dish need only consist of at least two separately pre-cooked parts, usually fried, that subsequently have been baked together. Its most constant constituent over time and space has been eggplant, whose affinity for olive oil is as celebrated in the East as it may be notorious in the West. Indeed eggplant is the obvious protagonist in the genesis of *mousaka*.

Originally *mousaka* had no structure at all. Its name is Arabic, and in Arab lands *mousaka* usually is not a layered dish, but rather a sort of vegetarian baked 'wet' chili: eggplant and onions are fried in olive oil, and then chick-peas and more oil are added before baking. Truly its place is with the amorphous *ladera*. Greeks of the eastern Aegean islands close to Anatolia make a dish along those unstructured lines, but it is not baked – and not called *mousaka*, either. Baking is definitional in any kind of *mousaka*.

Architecture came to *mousaka* with ground meat, whose introduction suggested layering the dish before baking. This certainly must have happened at least by around 1800 since Ami Boué, the early 19th century explorer of Ottoman Europe, mentioned *mousakou* [sic] as "a ragout of chopped mutton with sorrel, and sometimes currants and aromatic herbs." Layering also opened the sluice for improvisation, particularly as *mousaka* moved further afield during Ottoman times and reached the northern Balkan lands where the olive does not grow and eggplant was unknown until nearly the 20th century. Some northern Balkan versions bear only the most tenuous family resemblance to the pan-Hellenic *mousaka* now identified almost universally as the only authentic kind. Variations can still be encountered even in Greece, especially in the north, but in almost any region seasonally (though never in kitchens that cater to tourists seeking authenticity). In one rustic Greek recipe, beans substitute ground meat between the eggplant slices, a combination that recalls the Arabs' proto-*mousaka*.

The familiar custard cap is a mark of *O Megas Mousakas* (i.e., *Le Grand Mousaka*). This superstructure also undergirds those who maintain that *mousaka* could reflect elements of Byzantine cuisine that were preserved by monastic communities and the wealthy classes. White sauce after all was invented by the ancient Greeks; and the possession of such lush skills is only reinforced by Boué's early 19th century notation that "the *blanc-manger* [sic], in Greek *thiason*, is not much known [in the Balkans] outside the refined Greek kitchen." The custard overlay on *mousaka* probably spread to other Balkan lands coextensively with the spread of the Greek emigrant commercial classes and their taverns. Thus, while even at our late date a custard roof is optional in the broadest definition of layered *mousaka*, a topmost pouring of at least a yogurt-and-egg mixture is deemed a mark of tradition in most Balkan eyes.

Hippocrates surely would not recognize *mousaka*. Classical lineage nonetheless is not out of the question. For in addition to white sauce the ancient Greeks also knew the frying pan, ground meat and sweet spices; and they considered olive oil supremely receptive to spices and herbs. What is more, according to one of Plutarch's dining companions (*Table-talk*), the ancient

Mainland Greece

Greeks had become rather undemocratically clever at concocting sloppy dishes:

> "The custom of distributing portions of meat was abandoned when dinners became extravagant; for it was not possible, I suppose, to divide fancy cakes and Lydian puddings and rich sauces and all sorts of other dishes made of ground and grated delicacies; these luxurious dainties got the better of men and the custom of an equal share for all was abandoned."

In none of its manifestations, not even in the few remaining ones that go topless, is *mousaka* a finger-food.

Olive oil puddles are natural to *mousaka*. Aficionados advise taking to them with bread even before piercing the custard with a fork. In its puddles may be read the entire history of a *mousaka*. As this history can span upwards of a week, the reward is greater than in the case of the true *ladera* dishes, which as a rule neither improve at all with age nor have any shelf life. However, a movement is underway among some less unctuous Greek chefs to see to the mopping up of the puddles before the plate ever reaches the table, or even to forestall their drip by eschewing extravagance in the early stages of *mousaka* assembly. Avid bread-eaters will be sent diving for margarine.

For the bibulous diner all other issues with respect to *mousaka* necessarily drown in the question of which

Greek Salad

wine to drink with it. The simplest solution is the one blandly offered by the great connoisseurs of wine, who have lumped *mousaka* with the great meatloafs and assigned it to the lower middle rank of dishes (the masterpieces of an earlier age are condemned to become the banalities of a later one). These commentators advise drinking with *mousaka* either *retsina* or third-rate wines of color, in either case to chase the olive oil. But this view, mired as it is in a lack of appreciation of olive oil's contribution to aromatic savor, fails alike the friend of wine and the friend of *mousaka*. At the very least, a Hippocratic approach to prescriptions for the combination of *mousaka* and wine is in order:

Now, fresh baked *mousaka* has not geled in either consistency or flavor and should be followed by young wines of mild flavor served cool; conversely, half-baked connoisseurs must at all costs avoid aged red wines and overheating themselves. *Mousaka* is most easily digested when it is 2- or 3-days old, at which time soft and aromatic white wines at cool-room temperature are to be recommended; but once mellowing is noticed in the imbiber, further quaffing should be curtailed lest the beneficial effects of this treatment be ground down. The gastronomic potential of *mousaka* generally peaks at 3 to 5 days, at which point fat wines are exercised in their aromatic properties and middle-aged diners will sit still and gush; however, if reheated more than twice, *mousaka* can suffer oven stress and acquire a smoky by-taste that calls for either tannic young red wine or oxidized white wine in order to suppress sympathetically morbid reactions in the diner. *Mousaka* either 1-day-old and cool or more than 5-days old and warm needs only plain wine.

18

HIGH WATER MARKS

I have sat here before on the *plateia* of Makrinitsa, high above the Thessalian port of Volos and the Pagassitikos Gulf. It was eight years ago. I did not plan on returning today. I am staying at Nea Anchialos, along the coast south of Volos, and my sole intent was to enjoy the village's wine, which enjoys a modest reputation because of a seawater savor imparted by the Aegean. But this morning when the couple who own the hotel there asked if I might like a lift into Volos with them, I was instantly overcome by a desire to revisit the mountainous Pelion peninsula, and to have another plate of *spetsofaï*.

My earlier visit was in the blissful days before it ever occurred to me to resort to my taste buds as a sort of compass and follow them to places, like Nea Anchialos for instance, known for a kind of wine or cheese or dish. I had been in a quandary as to where to stop off for three days of relaxation on my way north to USDA meetings in Bulgaria. The cousin of a Greek friend in Athens was working in a travel agency and advised me to try Pelion, the touristic gem of Magnisia. I was told of scenic delight, idyllic bathing and also, I well remember, the local food specialty bizarrely tagged *spetsofaï*. A warning of Plutarch about flatterers dragging people off to baths and having them order novel dishes flashed through my mind, but I was sold just the same.

I had been staying with my friend's family in Athens and was anxious to set out on my own. Twelve years had elapsed since my first visit to Greece and I wanted to put to use the Greek I had been learning on my own the previous five years. I found out on the bus from Athens to Volos that it would not be easy. The man seated beside me persisted in trying to converse by using his twenty or so words of English rather than let me have a crack at Greek. I did not know then, as I know so well now, that Greeks usually are more determined to avoid speaking Greek to a foreigner than I am to speak Greek to them. I gave up on my bus companion to Volos shortly after we passed Thermopylae.

My ascent of Pelion began early in the afternoon in the dingy bus depot of Volos, where I bought a ticket for Makrinitsa, the Peliorite village that my friend's cousin especially recommended. The ticket assigned me to a specific, numbered seat on the bus, but that was not going to impress my fellow passengers, Peliorites and Greek tourists all. The boarding scene was pandemonium itself from the moment the destination sign was raised above the bus's windshield. Young women ran over old ones; old folks knocked away youngsters; and the children, taking their cue from their elders, pushed over other people's baggage to scramble aboard. I was so flustered by it all that I

Greek Salad

made the ultimate mistake of acting aloof, which is always execrable in provincial Greece when boarding any means of public conveyance; for every Greek knows that a seat number on a ticket is only ink on paper and that possession is all of carriage law. And in the heat of the contest my Greek vocabulary failed me. Finding a mustachioed man ensconced in my assigned place, I mutely showed him my ticket with that seat number on it. In response he simply emitted a "Bah!" (which as I could understand from the body language of his shrug, translated as "So, what?"), and went right on sitting. That brief exchange cost me my shot at the couple of remaining seats at the rear of the bus. I stood all the way up to Makrinitsa.

The travel agent in Athens had assured me there would be no shortage of lodgings on Pelion at that time of year, around the middle of September, when the tourist season was waning. Nevertheless, I had learned a valuable lesson at the Volos bus depot, and upon arrival in Makrinitsa I snatched up my suitcase and got a head start over the other passengers, whom I left behind sorting out their multiple belongings in the village's parking lot. Just within the village proper an old two-story stone dwelling with the distinctive Pelion flagstone roof was serving as a guest house, and I was offered a room that was coziness itself, if one enjoys being enveloped by shaggy sheepskin *flokati* rugs and carved folk furniture. Seduced by flattery in the first place, I saw no reason to demur once on Pelion. I was told that the room was the last one available, and I grabbed while the grabbing was good.

I think my decision to come to Pelion that first time figures as a watershed event in my life. Even though I did not come here primarily for the sake of *spetsofaï*, my having considered the dish at all was, back then, remarkable. Yet my real moral collapse came on Pelion itself, where I paid no heed to Plutarch's antidote to flattery – that we should take more pride in abstinence than in enjoyment – whenever a rare and notorious luxury is afforded us. The fact was, I was going to attend to *spetsofaï* at the earliest opportunity.

I got out and about right away to pass the hours until dinner. A pack of children, some of them resident and some of them just vacationing, took an interest in my camera, accent and origin, and they attached themselves to me on my self-conducted tour. It was a great opportunity to practice Greek at the grass roots level, since not even the oldest of the children had as yet been touched by a desire to know English. The children and I inspected remnants and ruins from Makrinitsa's far more industrious and prosperous times in the 18th and 19th centuries, when Pelion enjoyed a large export trade in dyed cloth. We also climbed up to a mountain plateau called Leshani, which one of the native children said is where the villagers grow most of their wine. The scene at Leshani must have been far different a century earlier, because its vineyards were too few and scraggy to intimate any vinous flattery for the palate nowadays.

When I returned to my quarters I met another lodger in the hallway, a Greek woman who together with her child was spending the warm months keeping cool on Pelion while her husband stayed down in Volos most of the time working. With evening fast approaching I was starting to get serious about *spetsofaï* and asked her whether any particular cooking establishment in the village was to be preferred for its rendition of the dish. The woman mentioned two places in Makrinitsa but gave her special nod to a *taverna* in Portaria, which had been the first stop made on Pelion by the bus from Volos. But she cautioned me that *spetsofaï* is a "burning" meal that I should not attempt to eat after sundown. In English that was plainly more practiced than my Greek, she explained that her husband had tossed and turned all night after having eaten *spetsofaï* one evening on his last visit.

Being young and gastro-intestinally brash, I was not deterred by the woman's warning. But neither was I going to set out back to Portaria. I had had enough of buses and hikes for one day. More to the point, I was still but a fledgling eater who would make no great strides on account of a super-duper recipe. Makrinitsa would have to suffice. But I did pass up a comfortable restaurant mentioned by the woman, and on my own reconnoitering chose a cramped and bare bones *taverna* where one could fear that the real thing would be dished out. It was this very *taverna* where I am presently sitting, except that now it is under new ownership.

Nothing so well demonstrates my newness to gastronomic traveling eight years ago as the fact that neither in speaking to the Athenian travel agent nor to my fellow lodger did I think to ask just what *spetsofaï* is. I could not have been more surprised to find, instead of a notorious novelty, a dish very similar to a basic one that was in my own limited repertoire of recipes (the flavor differences between the two would only have interested palates used to far more stroking than mine was). *Spetsofaï*, it turned out, consists of pieces of local Peliorite goat-and-sheep-meat sausage (the chief divergence from my recipe) simmered with tomato and green pepper in olive oil. In sum, it was no more flattery than that to which I could have treated myself at home for a lot less trouble, and the *taverna* had no wine from Leshani to wash the *spetsofaï* down with, either, only some bottles from distant parts of Greece. As for the dish's 'burning' nature, I did detect some red pepper, but the sensation was so slight that anyone comfortable with even mildly 'hot' foods could have relished it for breakfast. I slept like a baby.

Bathing had also been part of the Pelion package presented by my friend's cousin and I fully intended to avail myself of that pampering as well. In fact I had prepared in Volos by purchasing mosquito repellant. (The pharmacist kindly accommodated my Greek and helped my progress by pointing out that I had asked for protection against cauliflowers – *kounoupithia* – rather than mosquitoes – *kounoupia*.) But Makrinitsa is not near a beach, and the children I met recommended Tsangarades on the far side of Pelion fronting the Aegean proper. Wanting to stay the night there, I checked out of my room in Makrinitsa. But once arrived in Tsangarades I learned that return buses were few and erratic. I felt there was a real possibility that I could miss the train connection from Salonica to Sofia for my business appointments, and so I returned from Tsangarades that same day without so much as getting my feet wet, let alone having to protect them from any sort of flora or fauna.

It was at this point in my earlier visit to Pelion that an unaccustomed sort of question visited me. It happened when I caught a glimpse of Portaria from the bus back to Makrinitsa and remembered that my informant at the guest house said the worthiest preparation of *spetsofaï* was to be had in a *taverna* there. I now wondered whether I should have settled for the dish in Makrinitsa. Thus caught up in the true gastronomic spirit, I remained on the bus and continued on to Portaria.

Portaria did not feel much different than Makrinitsa. But I was struck by the contrast between the Spartan steel-frame bed I took in Portaria and the charming wooden one I had left behind in Makrinitsa. The Portaria hotel itself, which had been built to serve as one, was from an earlier era of travel and for a hardier sort of traveler. I was attracted to it by the sight of a very old man seated out front beside a single small table. He made no effort to coddle me with my own language and was far keener to tell me about the merits of Portaria's various spring waters than to check me in. His simplicity moved me to engage a room without looking further for more up-to-date accommodations. Besides, the room was absolutely spotless and the sheets whiter than white.

The old man's talking point was a photograph from decades back in which he was to be seen among a group with the King of Greece in front of the very same hostelry during a royal rest at Portaria. The King had come on account of Pelion's renowned spring waters, which are especially numerous and excellent in and around Portaria and Makrinitsa. I must admit that I had grown complacent about water years before that still early time in my life. Indeed, I felt about water much as did Epicharinus, who declared, "There can be no dithyramb when you drink water." Winebibbers have long since forgotten that the font of our vocabulary for speaking about wine was in the hotel-keeper's pre-Dionysian penchant to distinguish the properties of various waters.

I found the recommended *taverna* in Portaria and ate what did seem to me a more painstaking version of *spetsofaï*. I also got a measure of Peliorite red wine that did not transport me to winy dithyrambs, though it was no watery liquid. I supposed it must have been different in the early 19th century when Pelion's vineyards were flourishing and its wine was praised by Western visitors. Plutarch after all attributed the best wines to the same sort of land from which the best spring waters arise. As I downed my first glass of Peliorite wine, however, I had to salve my palate with the thought that there is only so much fine wine an unflattered body can take, which perhaps is an obtuse way of understanding what Plutarch meant when he said, "Some people feel most impelled towards wine when the drink they most want is water."

Today I stopped off in Portaria for a while before coming back here to Makrinitsa for lunch. The old hotel was spiffed up, but the ancient mariner of Pelion waters was gone from his post. He has probably been carried off on the flow of the Styx by now.

I don't know what I might have been expecting in returning to Pelion. I have advanced so far in gastronomy that I am reading Brillat-Savarin's *The Physiology of Taste* as I travel. Certainly nothing written by that seminal gastronomic philosopher could have encouraged me, for he had no appreciation whatsoever of water ("water awakens no sensation of taste"). I felt sorry for him that he had not come to Pelion and met someone like the old hotel-keeper.

Anyway, it has done me good to sit here in the balmy tranquility I find under the plane trees of

Mainland Greece

Makrinitsa and, in my gastronomic maturity, look at *spetsofaï* anew. I have been able to put out of my mind the cacophony of persuasion in favor of luxury food and wine, and to contemplate the graffiti I spotted on the retaining wall today along the road from Portaria to Makrinitsa: "May your sight have meaning, not that which you look at." Brillat-Savarin could not have put it better in one of his aphorisms, and the ring of truth is as sonorous as the sound of Pelion's waters gurgling ever downward below the *plateia*.

19

TO TASTE A GREEN STONE

It's usual in Greece to skip the merely quaint while hurrying off to antiquities. I've done it myself, like the time I passed up Arachova on the way to Delphi. How could a little mountain town in the heart of Central Greece compete with the site which was for the ancients the navel of the world?

Arachova sits high up the flank of Mount Parnassos in Boeotia, about two-and-a-half hours west of Athens by car, on or near an ancient settlement called Anemolia, or 'Windswept,' (because, related the geographer Strabo, "squalls of wind sweep down upon it"). Anemolia apparently developed partly to supply the needs of pilgrims to the Delphic Oracle. But present-day Arachova did its growing during Ottoman times, when families of means abandoned the more easily harassed lowlands. Anyway, the place preserves the rusticity of Central Greece with exceptional authenticity, notwithstanding the steady steam of tourist buses through it. Yet I did not dally that first time I laid eyes on Arachova. True to touristic form, I made haste for Delphi.

It was not until five years later that I gave so much as a thought to Arachova. I was at that time sent delving into my faint recollections of the place by its mention in a recent travelogue as a producer of dry red *brousko* wine. Good *brousko* is nothing to pass up, but even so, I had no thought of following a lead on a village that does not bottle any wine. Arachova once again left me in peace.

But two years later I found myself in Athens on a business trip, and while thinking one Saturday about what to do with the Sunday open to me, I noticed an announcement in the hotel lobby for a bus tour to Delphi the next day. Much as I hate to waste precious time in Greece retracing my steps, it occurred to me to see about going with the tour bus only as far as Arachova. The hotel desk clerk, as though thinking Arachova populated by preposterously bucolic folk, seemed highly amused by my plan. But she assured me that it could be arranged, and she in fact saw to it.

But actually getting off the bus in Arachova took some doing. The tour guide, who had been duly apprised to expect such a passenger, was most reluctant to accept the proposition when faced with the corpus. As we approached the village she tried to persuade me that I would wear out Arachova within an hour's time, and not even my protestation that I had already done Delphi could dissuade her from her opinion that I would find far more of interest there than in Arachova. Finally there was nothing to do but confess and simply tell her that I wanted to taste some wines. She was literally dumbstruck by my announcement, and in the interval during which she tried to make sense of what

Greek Salad

she had just heard, I came to the realization that must come sooner or later to all who travel in pursuit of fermented grape juice: My passion is not readily comprehensible to all and sundry, and sometimes should be kept to myself at all costs.

The guide recovered herself for one last appeal to reason, but at last relented, and we made the necessary arrangement for my retrieval later in the day. The apostate from the Delphi tour was ignominiously dumped out beside the refuse containers of an Arachovite café.

I wasted no time in setting about inquiring after *brousko*. A sympathetic pensioner sitting at the café was anxious to help me but explained that Arachova did not have much wine these days owing to a sharp decline in vineyard area since the Second World War. However, he introduced me to another café-sitter, a vineyard owner. This fellow had no *brousko* left that mid-September day and said that I should have been there in the spring when he had quite enough. We walked to his cellar anyway so that he could give me a glass of another wine. I was surprised by its pinkish color – hardly what I expected of Arachova – and when I tasted it I noticed that it had oxidized a bit. I thought poorly of it though I managed to grin satisfaction.

We parted company at the cellar door and I climbed from there up to the Church of Ayios Yeoryios (the patron saint) at the top of this steep settlement. The long series of steps is the scene each St. George's Day of 'the old men's race,' when Arachova's numerous and spry octogenarians and nonagenarians compete in getting up to the church first. Just behind the churchyard I discovered 'Panayota's Tavern,' a small indoor establishment presided over by an elderly but robust couple. I announced my purpose in coming to Arachova and was again disappointed to hear that the red wine was gone. They said I should come back the following spring.

But they did have their *retsina*, and a correct one it was. Along with it they brought me a bowl of a mutton-and-potato stew that was being served to a table of Arachovite customers. On top of that came a glass of a second wine. This wine was four-years-old and of light onion-skin color, and I realized that it was a mature version of the sort of wine that I had endured earlier at the cellar. It was eminently palatable.

I tried to pay for the unexpected hospitality but was refused. I knew that none of the visitors to Delphi were having that experience.

After excusing myself from the company at Panayota's I found my way up the side of Parnassos, with my goal the highest vineyard parcels. This took me quite high, and nearly into the dense clouds that were coming in over Parnassos. From this vantage I could look all the way down the Pleistos Gorge and the sea of olive trees leading to the Gulf of Corinth. I could also see all about me the traces of what had once been hundreds of hectares of vineyards.

A species of super-gnat possessed of incredible buzzing powers was more of a nuisance than Strabo's swooping squalls of wind, and caused me to have my fill of scenery before my eyes tired of it. I made my way back down into the same lane where I had started out, but at a point farther along. There I came upon what looked like another *taverna*, though it did not announce itself as such. I went inside, where I found only some members of the family running the place present, all of them at work off to the side in the open kitchen typical of these establishments. Once more I gave my explanations only to be told that they, too, had run out of *brousko*.

But they still had some red – not merely rosy – *retsina*. As I sat tasting this most rare of vinous oddities, which even few Greeks know exists, who should come in the door but a short and stocky man to whom I had been cursorily introduced just before I left Panayota's. I had assumed he was a habitué there because on his approach to the entrance he was wryly pointed out to me by the international thumb-to-mouth gesture. But he was home now, as it turned out, at his very own *taverna*. It was time for Sunday dinner. And to my great delight this proprietor ordered a place set for me. Every morsel passing our lips was produced right there on the Parnassos of the ancients, and as is the way in such circumstances, the thought only enhanced the natural flavorsomeness of everything. We continued through the meal with the red *retsina*, but I was of course invited back for spring to taste the unresinated *brousko*.

On the way back to the roadway I poked my head into an open cellar door where I could see a man at work. He too was out of red wine, but he spared me the invitation for spring. He did think, though, that I had a chance of finding a bit of *brousko* somewhere after everyone arose from their siesta. However, I had no more time for Arachova that day. It was time for me to be on my way to the rendezvous with the tour bus and to the next morning's business appointments in Athens.

The clouds over Parnassos turned to a hard rain, and I arrived quite wet at the shop where the bus sat while my fellow day-trippers were inside looking over the fur and woolen goods that Arachovite merchants sell to fleece the profane contemporary pilgrim to Delphi. The tour guide spotted me, came over and volunteered ebulliently that everyone had had an absolutely splendid time at Delphi. She wondered skeptically whether I thought Arachova had been worth it. Not having found what I had come to taste, I could hardly gloat, so I ignored the question and changed the subject. This yielded an elucidating piece of information, namely that the guide had resided by Tyson's Corner, not far from where I live, while attending Northern

Greek Salad

Virginia Community College. How could a Greek dipped in the Tyson's Corner Shopping Mall any longer appreciate Arachova or the fine points of *brousko*?!

Arachova dwelled on my mind after that visit. I wanted to find out what was under the taste, so to speak, of the resinated red wine. As I sank ever further into Greek wine I began mapping out a campaign through the country's vineyard regions for the following spring. There was no dearth of significant wine-producing places to consider visiting. I added and deleted destinations a hundred times in choosing among them. Only minor, non-bottling Arachova was a non-negotiable constant. Actually, it seemed to me in my lucid moments that the trip was just a massive cover-up for getting to Arachova while the *brousko* still flows. For had Zeus flung a thunderbolt and commanded me not to write a word about Greek wine, I still would have been off to Arachova. My intuition told me that I would find a liquid beauty if I made the search, and I have never thirsted after any wine the way I did that one.

Some of my ilk – the wine-mad – will ask in amazement, "Are you saying that you spent $2,000 to taste the red wine of Arachova?!" They will take out their pocket calculators and point out that for a mere thousand dollars more I could have had a whole case of Château Petrus '89 and would surely have learned more about wine from that. But is that any way to think?! Certainly some things are still beyond price. Some, like my proposed return to Arachova, fall under The Green Stone Principle that Zorba set it out when Kazantzakis chose not to come to Serbia to look at a "most beautiful green stone" that Zorba had unearthed there: "Here you had the chance of a lifetime to see a beautiful green stone and you didn't see it…There sure is a hell for certain penpushers."

I had hoped to arrive in Arachova for the Easter celebration, which that year fell late. As it turned out I did not get there until the Tuesday after Easter, but not much was lost since the Easter holiday overlaps Arachova's St. George's Day celebration. I arrived on the last of three days of combined festivities and found virtually everyone, including many returned emigrants, gathered in the churchyard.

A small chapel across from the church had been converted into a temporary pantry, where stacks of bread, mounds of the outstanding local *feta* cheese and spit-roasted Parnassos lambs were being prepared for serving. Working on the lambs was the pensioner whom I had met the previous September, and who now mentioned that formerly he was a butcher. Demijohns of wine were also sitting about, and after the rest of the catering crew was introduced I was given a cup of it to sample – resinated red. Then some of everything else was thrust into my hands. Soon all the attendees were gathered at the tables lined up in the churchyard and the food and drink were brought out. We all fell to it

Greek Salad

with a gusto I've only seen surpassed at buffet tables spread at sophisticated cosmopolitan gatherings at Washington embassies. The butcher got up to address a poem of his own composition to the half-listening throng, as he does each year.

Then the dancing started. It was a radiant day and the breezes were energizing, and I put down my cup and joined the chain. And what better place for it then Arachova? Parnassos anciently was visited every two years by the maenads (women 'mad' from wine) for bacchic gamboling.

Some of the dancers were in their seventies and eighties, though their prancing made most of the fifty-year-old bureaucrats I had left back home seem terribly ill. The band consisted of two hoary shepherds in well-worn local garb, the one playing a primitive drum and the other a fat wooden flute. And did they play. After the dance they walked all about the village playing, and they continued into the dark of evening at the several cafés. What stamina. Oh, but *how* that flutist played at the dance. The muses had run away with him and he reached some unfrequented plane, completely oblivious to everything outside himself and his instrument. He became one with the flute, and the two of them with the chair he was sitting on. The flutist, the flute and the chair were shaking violently, and I thought the three of them would drive themselves into the ground while the dancers spun their blurry circle round them.

Mainland Greece

But it was not dancing that I had come for. I broke away in the middle of the festivities and moseyed over to Panayota's to claim my spring glass of *brousko*. I was recognized, greeted and treated to a glass of rather light unresinated red wine. I headed further up the lane to see if the family I had met the previous year was on duty. I had not seen any of them at the fest and thought that perhaps they were doing a land-office business. But their place looked empty. Looking more closely, I noticed a large lump under a blanket on a bed in the far corner and could identify paterfamilias, whom I could only suppose had been partaking freely of *brousko* the past two days. I returned to the focal point of the afternoon and subsequently went all about Arachova with a helpful town clerk to sample wines where he thought we could find them. None of the reds met my grand expectations.

Persistence can count for a lot in tracking down wines at down-on-their-luck Greek wine places like Arachova, and so later in the evening I went once more to see my acquaintances at the second, apparently nameless *taverna*. This time all were present, including family members I had not met the past September. As we talked I found out that this was not a *taverna* at all, but only a home, although the cavernous room, the six or seven tables surrounded by chairs, and the large glass front gave quite a different impression. I thought that Mr. Kalivas, as the owner was called, either must be seeking ego compensation in his home

Greek Salad

(his name comes from the Greek for 'hut') or else does not care to speak about a failed business.

With my mind on his wine again, I asked Mr. Kalivas whether he is a general farmer, to which he replied that he has some vineyards, olive trees and animals, but that they are only for his family's needs. He does not make his living from farming. "I am," he continued, "a public employee. I pick up the trash, the refuse." I thought of all the paper plates, cups and lamb bones scattered about the village and could understand why Mr. Kalivas might choose to snooze through the goings-on rather than attend them.

I had been poured some unresinated red of no particular distinction, but as Mr. Kalivas answered my questions about his vineyard and winemaking I learned that this was his second-quality wine, which he gets by pressing the grape-skins after the 'free-run' juice has been obtained. I asked to taste his best, which is the wine from the free-run juice, and the woman of the house disappeared and returned shortly with a pitcher of another red wine. This wine was so far inclined toward blue that it vividly brought to life Homer's description of a "wine-dark sea." Its smell could have made me think that the vine used to produce it must be a successor to the ancient Greek "frankincense vine" mentioned by Pliny: "with a scent like that of incense, the wine from which is used for libations to the gods." Yet in favor of this *brousko* I really cannot do better than to quote from Plutarch in *The E at Delphi*:

Mainland Greece

"The fact is, Boëthus," said Sarapion, "that we are ailing both in ears and eyes, accustomed as we are, through luxury and soft living, to believe and to declare that the pleasant things are fair and lovely. Before long we shall be finding fault with the prophetic priestess because she sings to the lyre, and because she is not perfumed and clad in purple when she goes down into the inner shrine, and does not burn upon the altar cassia or laudanum or frankincense, but only laurel and barley meal."

Arachovite red may not be for soft living, but nothing is spared at its inner shrine.

I might now declare that at its best, as in 'Château Kalivas,' the *brousko* of Arachova is a most memorable wine. But whether or not Arachova has ever produced anything like Great Wine seems to me a moot matter. I can say also that I have extracted a lot from Arachova on the subject of wine – certainly more than I could from a case of Château Petrus '89 without imagination getting the better of my consciousness. Yet in the final tabulation I have no way of balancing my costs and benefits in having gone out of my way for Arachova. All that counts is that I went and saw my green stone.

20

PHOTO SYNTHESIS

My daughter has two matching postcards from Athens in the photo album she keeps of our trips to Greece. Both pictures were taken from the same direction and show the Temple of Olympian Zeus in the foreground and the Acropolis in the background, in the very same juxtaposition, as though the two photographers had stood on the very same blocks of ancient rubble. The one postcard is in color while the other is black-and-white. The other difference between them is 39 years.

I received the black-and-white in 1953, when I was six. My father sent it from the Navy cruiser *USS Des Moines* in the Mediterranean. I kept it in the desk where I did my schoolwork while I was growing up and would pull it out to pore over occasionally when my mind wandered from my studies. In 1963, when I was sixteen and going through some sort of broody hormonal crisis, I noticed a travel ad and asked my parents to let me go to the Mediterranean by myself aboard the Greek liner *TSS Olympia*, and in their frustration with me they decided to take a chance on the ship towing me out of my doldrums. Of course the *Olympia* was going to call at Piraeus, the ancient port of Athens.

Mainland Greece

The newer, color postcard was sent by my daughter to my father in 1992. She bought it in the old Plaka quarter that abuts the Acropolis, right after we visited the Parthenon. I had told her when she was seven or eight that I would take her to Greece someday. I was probably under the influence of *retsina* and *bouzouki* music at the time I made the statement, but children do not accept such excuses for failure to live up to what they think amounts to a promise, and my daughter never let me forget that one. I managed to stall on delivering only until she was fourteen.

*

My father regularly sent me postcards from his ship's ports of call, but the one from Athens somehow affected me more than the others. I think it appealed to my predilection for stone. I used to play among the chiseled headstones that my grandfather, a retired stonecutter, kept lined up like a miniature cemetery in the backyard. On my first return visit to Athens, in 1975, I had a Greek college friend take a photo of me in front of Cemetery A ('Necrotapheion Alpha') in the Neos Kosmos quarter where we caught a bus to the Temple of Olympian Zeus. Athenian cemeteries shine from alabaster and marble and have none of the gloominess of my grandfather's granite headstones. I like to think it is a carryover from antiquity ("brightness and honour belong to my yearning for the sun" – Sappho). But maybe Necrotapheion A simply imparts mournfulness in some other way that I don't pick up

Greek Salad

on. Anyway, I'm attracted to ancient Greek stelae as well.

*

Perhaps my favorite photo from Athens is one my daughter took of the Thesion in 1992. I wanted her to see the Thesion even before the Parthenon. The smaller scale and scented setting of the Thesion have always exerted more of an emotional impact on me than most other ancient sites do. When we visited Delphi that year we saw a woman standing with her eyes closed, head upward and arms outstretched as if trying to grasp for the ghost of the oracle, or at any rate for the spirit of the place, but I have always found as much of that sort of communing as I can cope with at the Thesion.

The Thesion was where my own sightseeing in Athens began in 1963. I was taken there by my Athenian host, Louie Sotirhos. I don't know what possessed him to show me an ancient temple. He had little taste for worship. I remember him spoofing his wife's religiosity and mimicking her at prayer as we walked to the electric train to go downtown from the suburbs. As if on cue to lend point to Louie's anti-clericalism, a priest boarded the train and took an impressive stance by one of the doors as if he were guarding the gates to Paradise. A Sunday school hush came over the cowed laity. Louie pursed his lips in a smirk and nodded his head to confirm my reading of the scene. Little wonder that he never took me to any Greek temples of the Christian era.

I have a photo from 1975 of an intersection by Apostolou Pavlou Street near the Thesion. It's close to where Louie and I got off the electric train. Before doing any sightseeing we sat down at a shaded café for 'Turkish coffee' (it was still called that in 1963). We were on a wedge of sidewalk between two sharply angled streets that converge on Apostolou Pavlou. Despite its location so close to a thoroughfare the spot has a tranquility that has drawn me back almost every time I've been in Athens. On my last visit the place was being gussied up and gentrified but had not lost its essential ambiance. I choked up a bit looking at the Acropolis and remembering that morning with Louie 32 years earlier, and suspecting I wouldn't be back for a long time. Fortunately, my daughter didn't notice and couldn't mock my irrational attachment to Athens. Unfortunately, unlike her photo of the Thesion, mine of that corner by Apostolou Pavlou captures nothing of its mood.

*

Louie sent me a formal, professional black-and-white photo of himself and his wife shortly after I returned home in 1963. Originally a countryman from Boeotia, he had become a U.S. citizen and acquired a taste for country-and-western music, which he associated with grass roots democracy, and a distaste for

Greek Salad

Byzantine chants, which reminded him of hierarchical religion. Louie had been a cabin-mate of mine on the *Olympia.* He took me under his wing on the voyage and went so far as to tell people I was his nephew, lest anyone think me an easy mark for foul play. My mother, who had some trepidation about letting me go on my adventure, felt much better about it after meeting Louie just before sailing time. He gave her a tension-releasing laugh when he pointed to the life-preservers in the cabin and said, "See those? Good for nothing." I detect something of his cynical wit in his expression in the photo.

*

Dionysos Areopagitou Street bordering the Acropolis has its picturesque moments in the course of a day and the seasons, but I imagine few pictures are actually taken of it since cameras usually are trained across the street and upward at the Parthenon. The only photo I have of it is one my daughter took the July evening we had dinner at a rooftop restaurant around one corner along Areopagitou. We were with a Greek publisher friend, his wife and a translator of "light pornography" who was working on some writing of mine about Greek wine. We went through several courses and three bottles of wine as the Parthenon changed colors during the nightly sound-and-light show. But it was 1992 and things were getting ugly in the Balkans, and the translator delivered a postprandial lecture to me on an obscure point of Greek nationalism that came up in connection with the name of a Greek grape variety. It made me sorry I wasn't a writer of heavy porn. Thank heavens a rare Attic summer rain began to fall and the company broke up.

I was supposed to stay at a pension on Areopagitou my first time in Athens. The pension was operated by a friend of the owner of the *Olympia*, and the ship's trip directress had given me the address. But it was nearly 10 p.m. when the taxi from Piraeus reached Areopagitou, and the pension maid who had the room keys had gone home for the night. I thought I had better come back the next day to claim my room beside history and in the meantime go and consult my recently acquired Greek uncle. I handed the taxi-driver the slip of paper Louie had given me with his address on it in case I needed help. I never got back to Areopagitou that trip and have no idea how differently I might view Athens now had I been headquartered next to the Acropolis then.

A photo that was not taken on Areopagitou but that I nevertheless associate with it shows the sulfurous cloud of pollution that nowadays periodically takes up residence over the Attic basin where contemporary Athens sprawls. My daughter took it from aboard a ferry in the Saronic Gulf late one afternoon as we were returning to Piraeus from the Cyclades in 1993. That same evening we had a table on the sidewalk at a *taverna* down another street off Areopagitou, and the city was so enveloped by stagnant dense air, that on one mouthful I tasted nothing but trapped exhaust fumes. I recall nothing like that from 1963, and I harbor the conceit that I was able to visit the Acropolis before the original caryatids on the Erechtheion had to be removed indoors and replaced with replicas. I keep quiet about it because the truth is I don't really notice the difference.

*

She may disagree, but as far as I'm concerned the best photo of my daughter from our Athens visits is one taken at the 11th century Kaisariani Monastery on Mount Hymettus. That was on our last trip together, in 1995. I had long put off visiting Kaisariani and wanted to be sure my daughter had the chance to see it too. Besides, it was virtually a straight shot by bus from our lodgings near the Hilton hotel to the end of the line where the hike up to the monastery begins. While there, a huge fire that was to last several days began among the pines on the far side of Hymettus, and thin clouds of smoke were just beginning to waft in over the mountain as we finished touring. We had already taken the picture I like so well. My daughter was seventeen and the play of light and shade across her unselfconscious pose while seated in the monastery courtyard reveals a girl on the verge of womanhood. It had been a classically brilliant Attic day, around noon, when hard truths cannot be hidden from the eye without subterfuge.

Mainland Greece

*

I have a prosaic shot of Constantinidou Street in the working-class suburb of Kato Patissia where Louie's family lived. The photo was taken late in the afternoon when the street was deserted because people had yet to emerge from their midday nap. Looking at it now I find it hard to believe the place was actually part of Athens. The street was as yet unpaved and street lighting was poor. Kato Patissia seemed practically a village. Constantinidou was also remote, and the night I arrived there in 1963 the taxi-driver succeeded in finding it only with a lot of what sounded to me like Greek oaths, and finally a stop for directions at a police precinct station.

Another photo features the plain front of the *taverna* operated by Louie's sisters. The family dwelling was attached to the rear of the building. It had five rooms and was occupied by Louie and his wife, and his two sisters and their husbands. I slept on a bed placed for me in the courtyard (Louie said it never rains in Athens in August). Early the first morning, his sisters dragged the bed, with me on it in a bewildered state, from the sun into the shade. I really felt I was inconveniencing the family, but when I said as much to Louie later in telling him of my intention to return to the pension on Areopagitou, his pride was so obviously wounded that I lost all resolve in resisting his hospitality. I slept drily outdoors the next four nights too.

Greek Salad

One of Louie's sisters is standing behind a stack of bread loaves in a picture taken right after their delivery to the *taverna* one morning. That particular kind of bread looked like an overweight *baguette*, with a truly golden brown crust and a dense texture extremely well suited to olive oil either straight, as on Greek salad, or in cooked dishes. But it has disappeared entirely from the Athenian repertoire of bread dough, apparently a victim of the standardization of flour formulas that was ushered in after Greece joined the European Union in 1981. Still, there are worthy breads to be had in Athens now too, for instance from an exceptionally versatile bakery we frequent near the U.S. Embassy. We have no pictures of the Embassy, just the bakery.

*

Our favored bakery does a good *tiropita*, the savory Greek 'cheese-pie.' *Tiropita* remains the ubiquitous Athenian snack, just as its ancient predecessor was (judging by classical literature). I recall walking in downtown Athens with two Greek employees of the U.S. Embassy one morning in 1982, and the one would point out to the other every so often, "Stamati, they have good cheese-pie there." I especially think of *tiropita* when looking at our picture of an ancient statue of a lion in Mesoyeia, the region of Attica southeast of Athens. We were shown the lion by Roxani Matsa, grower of a classic Attic white wine (without resin). She said the locals snicker about the statue because it rests at a tilt, with the lion's butt thus raised rather suggestively upward (Attic humor obviously has not changed over the millennia either). Back at her estate Roxani was going to serve us a *tiropita* of her own making to show off her wine the better, but her house cat had dived into it face first and ruined it while we were away chuckling about the other feline.

*

Louie and his family were long gone from Athens and settled in Seattle by the time I started taking my daughter to Greece in the 1990s. She and I stayed at rooms I found on Evzonon Street in the fashionable Kolonaki quarter near the Hilton hotel during the intervening years. Evzonon is conveniently located for sightseeing, and my daughter is enamored of the better-than-home bathrooms we have there. What is more, Evzonon is a quiet street, which is remarkable in central Athens. The most distracting sounds are the morning clanging of bells at the small Byzantine chapel across the street, and the uncanny evening yodeling of the ancient mutt who loiters perpetually in front of our building. We have photos of both the chapel and the mutt.

My daughter also likes that our quarters on Evzonon give ready access to two veritable temples of oriental pastry. One of them is located cattycorner to an erstwhile restaurant from where I snapped a downhill shot of Loukianou Street, on the flank of Lycabettus hill in Kolonaki, in 1983. When I look at the picture I

mostly think of the restaurant's kid dishes and remarkably eclectic selection of Greek wines. But my
sweet-toothed young traveling companion associates
the scene only with the chocolate *baklava* she gets at
the pastry shop a few steps uphill. She relishes afternoon pastry pick-me-ups. I think of my first afternoon
after siesta on Constantinidou when Louie threw open
the shutters with fanfare ("See – air condition!") and
poured *ouzo* and glasses of cold water.

A rather artistic picture taken by my daughter
shows a lone man seated at a *taverna* in Plaka. The
taverna served outstanding stuffed grapevine leaves –
the leaves were home-grown and firm, and the *avgolemono* (egg-lemon) sauce was supple. The prospect
of meals like that draws us to Athenian *taverna*s more
often than to restaurants. Once while strolling in Kolonaki before dinner we took a look at a pretty restaurant that had recently been selected as tops in the city
for its innovative Greek-style dishes, but we had cold
feet about eating there after studying and speculating
about the descriptive menu. We ended up at a *taverna*
where even the well-heeled denizens of Kolonaki retreat for simplicity.

*

Lycabettus isn't far from Evzonon, and we were
very glad of it the day we visited a big wine firm in
Mesoyeia in 1992. Expecting to be back in Athens by
lunch, we'd had only a token breakfast. But we ended

Mainland Greece

up far off in Boeotia at the firm's new winery, which had all the allure of a soybean processing plant (our picture of it shows two guard-dogs at their respective doghouses on either side of the entrance gate). More to our liking was a family-run winery in Mesoyeia where we stopped beforehand. The wine maker stands out in our group photo there. Compact and tousle-haired, and wearing only short-shorts and sandals, he was the next best thing to a satyr. He was also more suited to Greek than foreign grapes – or at least I preferred his *retsina* to his cabernet. Later in Boeotia my daughter and I commiserated about passing up his wife's offer to fry eggs fresh from her hens. Famished by the time we got back to Evzonon, we dashed over to the funicular for Lycabettus and made straight for the restaurant at the top. We took the staff by surprise by the earliness of the hour and ate heartily with the city spread out before us in the late-day light. Athens looked especially good and we took a picture from our table. The Acropolis was magnificently dead center in our field of vision.

*

A picture from 1995 shows me with Louie's sisters, their nephew and his wife at the nephew's apartment in the tree-lined suburb of Maroussi. The sisters were sojourning from Seattle. I hadn't seen them in over twenty years and we visited them several times. My daughter made friends with the nephew's daughter, her contemporary and a fanatic devotee of a Greek

Greek Salad

rock star whose pictures are plastered all over the wall in back of us in the photo. We're seated at the dining room table prior to a meal of baked kid that the sisters made for us. I was grateful to the nephew for troubling to find some village *retsina* the likes of which I hadn't tasted in years, maybe not since my stay in Kato Patissia three decades earlier.

The only photo of me in Athens on my first visit shows me standing among wine barrels in the *taverna* on Constantinidou. I had one of Louie's sisters take it the morning the *retsina* was delivered. I had become a fan of the stuff at the welcome-home party for Louie the night the *Olympia* reached Piraeus. *Retsina* was always on the table at lunch and dinner. Over a glass of *retsina* Louie would sprinkle mealtime conversation with anecdotes from various periods of Greek history extending from the Trojan War to his own experiences on the Albanian front during the Second World War. He always included tidbits from popular memory – or else popular imagination – that I am sure are not recorded by historians. It was after a patchwork discourse of his late one evening that Louie sent me up on the roof of the house to see the floodlit Acropolis in the distance. That remains my favorite memory of the site.

I regret having no photo of myself in front of the Parthenon from that first visit. I would like to be able to place it beside my daughter's in her album. Louie took me to the Acropolis, of course. But when we reached the entrance he was outraged to find that an admission fee had been instituted since he had last been there. Saying that the Acropolis "belongs to all the people," he refused to buy a ticket for himself though he did for me. I'm sorry I didn't press him to come along. Not only would I have had my picture taken, but I also would like to have heard Louie's narrative about the caryatids.

21

LANGUAGE LAB

Re gamoto!

Twenty-five years of trying to learn Greek and the experience boils down to an everyday expression that is still, practically speaking, Greek to me. It is one of those expressions that has no precise English equivalent, is not touched by Greek-English dictionaries and is not taught at Berlitz.

I only came to grips with *re gamoto* recently in fact, while in the Peloponnesos, unlikely place for it though it might seem. We had positioned ourselves at the town of Nafplion, at the seaward end of the Argive plain, in order to do some heavy classical touring – Mycenae, Tiryns, Argos, Epidauros. Agamemnon and Clytemnestra, Menelaos and Helen – all the storied Hellenic names crossed my mind while we were at Nafplion. Yet it was this dubious demotic expression that really grabbed hold of me.

It started the very first morning, when I took our Walkman with me onto the balcony of our hotel room while my daughter dressed. I was going to brush up my Greek listening comprehension after being away for a year. My ears had whatever it is that ears experience in the way of an 'eyeopener' when the first song came on. It was a male vocal, sung in an appropriately gravelly voice, and *re gamoto* was doing duty as a peevish refrain in it. I had thought the expression at least quasi-vulgar. Hearing it on the air made me think that Greek public standards for vulgarity might be collapsing under the amorphous influence of rap music.

But along the harbor promenade in Nafplion that same evening a couple in their thirties was strolling hand in hand when suddenly the man stopped dead in his tracks, threw his hands, palms out, down to his pelvis and invoked *re gamoto* while making a point to his ladylove. The couple looked every bit as staid as my own good self.

Usage Check: for venting utter frustration

My daughter chased me out onto the balcony in Nafplion at least three times daily during our weeklong stay while she suited up for touring, swimming or dining, as the case might be. The balcony afforded a grand view over the gulf at anytime of day, but no space to spare, and I was penned up there for twenty minutes at a stretch. Never mind the Walkman and the chance to listen to radio ads in Greek for electrical appliances on sale on the Argive plain, I was really feeling put out about it: "*Re gamoto*! Why the hell can't you change in the bathroom, like me?"

Greek Salad

Twenty-five years may seem a long time not to have incorporated a fairly common expression into my active vocabulary. My excuse is that most Greeks, as soon as they detect my accent, do not give me a chance to activate any of my vocabulary, and so, little of it becomes second-nature to me. Some think they are doing me a favor, in the way of hospitality, by accommodating me in my own language. Others merely want to strut their English, particularly when their compatriots are within earshot. But there has to be more to it. Although Greeks proclaim pride in the glorious past of their language, its marginal status today must be subconsciously humbling, indeed to the point that they presume it to be utterly useless to anyone not tied, as it were, umbilically.

My experience in Nafplion was blessedly better than average. Never before did the locals at large do so well in keeping their English under wraps for my benefit. An open-air vendor selling cold beverages near the head of the 899 stairs up to the Venetian fortress of Palamidi even gave me impromptu language lessons – a first during my travels in Greece – on the several occasions when we bought bottled water from him. I should have asked him about *re gamoto* while he was at it, but I did not know how he would take the question and thought he might stop dispensing his pointers.

Best of all was the friendship we made with Kosta Ioannides, an elderly shopkeeper whom we met while wandering in the alleys of the handsome old-town our second day. We visited and sat with him in his shop every afternoon after that, and he and I talked, in Greek, about historic Nafplion and the fruits of the fertile Argive plain, while my daughter examined costume jewelry and other craftwork, some of which had been made by Kosta himself. As an enthusiastic world traveler, he may have had some knowledge of English, but if he did he kept it from me.

Kosta was of a fine intelligence. In *Journey to the Morea* (Morea being a colloquial name for the Peloponnesos), Nikos Kazantzakis made the observation, while in Nafplion, that the apparent intellectual drowsiness of provincial towns paradoxically has produced many of the very individuals who have reinvigorated Hellenic culture, and particularly the Greek language, in recent times. Despite having been the first capital of modern, independent Greece, Nafplion was a languid backwater in the 1930s and remained that way until mass tourism induced a bright face-lift and an apparent straightening of the cerebral shoulders. Henry Miller, in *The Colossus of Maroussi*, used the occasion of his visit to the town, on the brink of the Second World War, to excoriate provincialism and provincials – but *he* was always satisfied to be in the company of urbane English-speaking Greeks.

Usage Check: for exaggerated or ironic congratulations

Greek Salad

Among his other talents Kosta was also a capable cook. He was avoiding red meat because of his high cholesterol count (it must be a positive sign that cholesterol-anxiety is reaching the Greek provinces), and one day he invited us back for the next day to try some of the eggplant spread he was going to make. We liked the spread so well that we asked for the recipe. Kosta gave it to us and also volunteered his recipe for ... tofu *mousaka*. 'Fusion cuisine' on the Argive plain?: "*Re gamoto*! Kosta, you old bugger! Tofu *mousaka*! What's next? Jicama *avgolemono*?!"

The usual Greek rebuff of my attempts to converse in Greek has infuriated me at times and made me feel I have wasted a lot of time during the past twenty-five years bothering with it. For the sake of my blood pressure I have learned to differentiate between the non-tourist sector, where I stand a chance of getting a hearing in Greek, and the tourist sector, where my chances are next to nil. As a rule I do not even attempt Greek in hotels or restaurants that make it their business to bend over backwards to cater to the presumed wishes of foreign visitors.

Our hotel in Nafplion was not quite world-class, but even so, the otherwise friendly and enthusiastic daytime clerk lacked all patience for slowing down his English to listen to my carefully measured Greek. However, since he was otherwise well-disposed, I eventually asked him, in English, whether *re gamoto* is not "dirty." He pursed his lips for a few moments and replied, with a coy grin, that it is and it isn't. This was, of course, of little help to me. I had always avoided using the expression for fear of mortally offending someone unintentionally. The only further clarification I got from the clerk was that it is not something you say when your mother is present.

It is not necessary to have a twenty-five year acquaintance with Greek in order to detect the origin that *re gamoto* shares with familiar words like mono-*gamy* and bi-*gamy*. The ancient Greek word for marriage was *gamos*. But while *gamos* was and remains consummately respectable in Greek usage, the fact that it all comes down to naked coupling plunged its *gam*-ic root into the arena of fornication as well. Yet for all of its inherent ribaldry the expression *re gamoto* has about it a certain impersonal quality, a kind of detachment, which sometimes allows it to be vocalized more or less benignly. In other words, it need not offend. But neither does this aspect of it translate, hence the non-native speaker's need for prudence.

The Greeks have been refining their obscenities for millennia (they were far ahead of us until at least as recently as Henry Miller). As far back as the 5th century B.C. the comic playwright Aristophanes was working on satisfying the Greek appetite for off-color language in the thespian arts. It was the period when Athenian comedy adopted from the Dorians ensconced in the Peloponnesos the use of ballooned phalluses and buttocks to give graphic emphasis to the regions whence so many of the jokes were coming. For example, here is Aristophanes in *The Congresswomen*, his play about a female plot to wrest government from the males:

Blepyros: This could turn nasty. We're not as young as we were, and with women in the driver's seat…Suppose they put the pressure on and coerce us.

Chremes: Into what?

Blepyros: Coerce us into coition.

Chremes: Screw *them*.

Blepyros: That's just what I mean.

Surely Aristophanes would not have shied from employing, for good effect, an early Greek expression corresponding to *re gamoto*.

Usage Check: for whispering under the breath in quiet desperation

One evening we duded up (I spent over half an hour on the balcony) and took a bus excursion from Nafplion for a performance of Aristophanes's play *Peace* at the ancient outdoor theater of Epidauros. The performance began with cannonades of Olympian flatulence and earthy talk about "dung-cakes." Since the performance was in modern Greek I had my ears pricked for an utterance of *re gamoto*, but if it ever came I missed it, just as much of the rest of the fast-paced and colloquial language sailed past my ears: "*Re gamoto*! Twenty-five years of work, all turned to crap by a lousy playwright. What a comedian."

Happily, Greek wine producers for some reason tend not to know English. Even though I have tried to become conversant in Greek across a broad range of conversation, I have progressed furthest with wine-speak. I can occasionally throw out a term so arcane that ordinary Greeks do not even know they have a word for it. That was how I spent much of the time that I should have been finding out about the parameters of handy expressions like *re gamoto*.

One English-ignorant wine producer is Epaminondas Spiropoulos, to whom we paid a visit on a day-trip south from Nafplion to Tripolis, the dreary capital of sylvan Arcadia. His winery is a short drive north of Tripolis, by the village of Artemision on the upland plain of Mantinia, the same plain where Epaminondas's namesake, the Theban general of antiquity, fell after his great victory there over the Dorians from Sparta.

The contemporary Epaminondas of my acquaintance has no grander strategy than to add to the pleas-

Greek Salad

ures of the Greek table with seductive Mantinian white and rosé wines. He draws inspiration from the hill near his winery on which the ancient city of Mantinia stood, and even more so from the fact that Pausanias mentioned a special precinct where Mantinians went to revel in "the orgies of Dionysus." Exactly how they took their bacchic enjoyment is a matter for speculation, but it seems a safe bet that it more often ignited profane couplings than sacred unions.

Gam-ey words and deeds must have been natural accompaniments to wine. Athenaeus, in *The Deipnosophists*, noted that Aristophanes referred to wine as "Aphrodite's milk" because, as Athenaeus put it, "quaffing too much of this, some conceive an appetite for illicit love." The wiser heads among the ancients regularly cautioned about wine and fornication, but the country folk did not always pay them heed. It is a rural scene that is depicted in Aristophanes's *Peace*, and the chief character in it is Trygaeus, who is named for the vintage (*trygos*) and has this to say:

> …ivy, new-wine strainers, bleating sheep, bosomy women jogging into the fields, drunken slavegirls, jugs of wine tilted skyward, and lots and lots of other blessings.

Aristophanian comedy and Doric phalluses, both became inseparably linked with Dionysian festivities.

Mainland Greece

Usage Check: for warding off the Evil Eye

An engaged couple stopped by the Spiropoulos winery to order wine for their wedding in the village. 500 guests would be attending! – and Epaminondas said this was not unusual. But if *gamos* is still a big draw in the Greek provinces, prenuptial coupling has come into play there as elsewhere. Which is why I am rethinking the wisdom of taking my daughter to Greece at her age. At lunch with the Spiropouloses she became preoccupied with one of the restaurant staff while I was absorbed with wine and Greek. I won't have busboys trying out their English on her before she has advanced beyond menu-Greek: "*Re gamoto*! Teenagers and their freaking hormones."

Conventional wisdom has it that the best way to learn a foreign language is to conjugate with a native speaker. I almost had the opportunity to find out whether this holds true for Greek as well. In fact my twenty-five year effort with the language is a relic from a Doric romance I once had.

I had been content in the early years of my infatuation with Greece to remain as superficially acquainted as Henry Miller was. I had no intention of learning Greek, either. Things took a lingual turn when I fell for a displaced Peloponnesian girl in Washington. She and I talked of a formal joining (that is, a *gamos* properly speaking), and also of living in Greece a while, so

Greek Salad

I decided to prepare for these immersions by learning Greek. But one day we had a falling out over what kind of pizza to order, and this caused her to rethink the whole relationship. She cited the pizza episode as evidence of irresolvable "cultural differences." This was undoubtedly true since at the time I didn't know *re gamoto* from oregano (*rigani*).

Because of my ill-fated amour with a Dorian it was a cruel irony that at the first meal in Nafplion my baked meat and gravy came on a bed of *hilopites*. These are only plain flat noodles, but "to eat the *hilopita*" is, in Greek, to say that you have been jilted. It would be stretching my cultural familiarity to pretend to know just how *hilopites* earned their role in the Greek passion play. The name means only 'mush-cakes,' and I cannot make much of that. I should not be surprised, though, if as a symbol of being told to kiss off they are but a proxy for Aristophanes's 'dung-cakes' (*kopropites*). My own romantic experience suggests, anyway, that "to eat the *hilopita*" is a surefire way to know the stuff of an impassioned ejaculation of *re gamoto*.

In Nafplion we visited a small-scale factory that was turning out *hilopites* by the bagful. *Hilopites* really do seem more popular in the Peloponnesos than in any other part of Greece. If you ask me, the original perpetrators of them were in all likelihood the Laconians, who in antiquity were a boorish bunch of Dorians with minimal culinary skills and even less gastronomic curiosity. The first batch of *hilopites* might well have been thrown together in the reign of Menelaos, when Helen ran off with Paris and left her Spartan king high and dry with his … well, I'm no Aristophanes.

In the pursuit of further cultural understanding, and the possible ancient linkage between some metaphoric noodles and a crypto-obscenity, I ought to have continued south from Tripolis and gone to Yithion on the Laconian coast to visit the offshore islet of Marathonisi that Helen and Paris used as their motel on their first night together. But we would have had to pass through Sparta, which happens to be where my former consort was from.

Kazantzakis wrote that Greeks frequently become gloomy when they travel in the provinces because they are confronted by the many sites where Greek fortunes went awry over the millennia. Even though I am no more Greek now than I was twenty-five years ago, I fear that I might become downright melancholic in Sparta if anyone *there* sets a plate of *hilopites* in front of me. And that is to say nothing of the fact that Sparta, because of the many Laconians who left for the States and came back to spend their retirement, is teeming with Greeks who speak English.

Greek Salad

Usage Check: as an oath prefacing a lethal thrust

"Argive Helen" must have had more culpability in her abduction than we usually give her credit for. It is Helen herself who tells us, according to Homer, of the hate her original husband, Menelaos, must feel for her. The way I figure it, the Trojan War had to have been launched with harsh words bellowed by Menelaos when he learned of Helen's elopement with Paris: "The bastard! He enjoys the hospitality of my palace and then wants my bed to boot! Man the ships! We'll drag that fair hussy back here, and I don't care how long it takes! *Re gamoto*!"

22

PIT STOP

I must admit to a vulgar predilection for Patras. I feel at home there in an almost nostalgic way that I can only attribute to my early years in Brooklyn. But few enough people even among the vulgar bother to make the acquaintance of Patras. It is the proverbial stopover on the way elsewhere. The city is situated at a bend along the coast of the northwestern Peloponnesos facing the Ionian Sea near the narrow western entrance to the Gulf of Corinth. Trips to the Ionian islands, Central Greece, Olympia and Corinth radiate from here. And nothing that can be seen of the city down where the ships, ferries, trains and buses converge is likely to entice anyone of fine sensibility to linger longer than necessary:

> I went down to the mole where the Patrians were hurrying to sip ouzo, munch loukoumi and listen to music…The sea simmered and reeked of rotten watermelon, tomatoes bobbed on the swell, mustachioed men cracked sunflowerseeds and spat far in the direction of the water.

(Kazantzakis, *Journey to the Morea*)

Patras is a workers' city. It's the genuine article too, not a sham like, say, the Communist-managed

Greek Salad

Bologna I saw, where a visitor might only infer prole-tarian sympathy from paraphernalia such as cutesy red stars on stylish caps, not from actual disposition. Come to think of it, the arcaded streets in some quar-ters give Patras the look of a down-at-the-heels Bolo-gna, or perhaps more aptly, in view of the port, a Sin-gapore of the Mediterranean. But it takes a measure of working-class nerve to mention Patras in the same breath as culinary meccas like Bologna and Singapore. The challenge of finding quality food and drink in Patras is daunting for anyone accustomed to relying on the certifications of gastronomic guidebooks and such. Few Patrians will tolerate the overhead for the fancy wrappings that make remarkable meals easy to find in more patrician places.

It was around noon the first time I came to Patras on the ferry from Central Greece – and my appetite had been growing since well before noon. I checked my bags at the bus depot along the waterfront and found a plain little restaurant that appealed to my ves-tigial Brooklyn fancy. For my meal I chose the day's special, a fricassee of kid, which was so good that even after my hunger pangs were quelled, it seemed to me a masterful rendition. Michelin will never know what they missed.

Water probably was more necessary to my condi-tion at the time than wine, but I was on wine safari and water with lunch was out of the question. But Patras's forte is sweet wine, both white Muscat and red Mavrodaphne, which not everyone will want to drink right when they are passing through. Lugging one's touring gear somehow usually works against the idea. (Plato may have been right in observing that honey "expands the contracted pores of the mouth to their natural condition." But did he carry his own baggage?) Fortunately, Patras also offers dry wines that meet the deceptive demands of a burning thirst. I ordered a light white one that was just the thing, next to water, for a hamal in heat.

The fricassee delivered that peculiar benefit of *cuisine proletarienne* – staying power. It left me in such good condition that I spent the entire afternoon on foot keenly looking over mile after mile of the city. Patras has, it must be pointed out, two distinct parts, an upper town and a lower town. The upper town is much the older part, indeed Antony and Cleopatra cavorted there. The graciousness that Patras was known for in the 19th century still peeps through on the high ground.

The old Patrian has associated his name with the rich well-traveled nobleman. The nobleman who knows how to live it up and rejoice in his days at the theaters, at social affairs, at the stroll on the pier…He knows how to appreciate the setting of the sun, the salt of the sea, the refreshing quality of the mountain, the fine wine…

(Alekos Maraslis, *Patra 1900*)

Greek Salad

The younger and meaner lower town gained the upper hand only in the 20th century, the age of the toiling masses, to the advantage of sunflowerseed-spitters.

I eventually reached the only Patrian landmark I was familiar with – from a wine label – the old Frankish fortress overlooking the port. Twilight was on the horizon by that time and the fricassee of kid was but a distant memory that could no longer fuel me. I held out as long as I could in the hope of spotting an upper-town restaurant with a touch of tablecloth class whose name I might mention sometime in polite company. But I finally gave in to advanced stirrings of hunger – and to my Brooklyn sensibilities – and headed directly for the staircases leading down to sea and sweat.

It did not take long in the lower town for me to be attracted to a *taverna*. Barrels of wine were lined up all along one side of the interior, and in the back of the establishment the proprietor was setting out pans of food. I was hooked the moment I caught a glimpse of the baked fish floundering in olive oil. The wine server took me for a crackpot when I wondered aloud whether the wine he brought was actually from the Achaian hills to the rear of town. I should not have expected that a visit to a lower town *taverna* would land me in any but Bolshevik company.

"…you spend all your time in the wineshops and the public houses, although the orator Isocrates has said in his *Areopagiticus*: 'No one, not even a

238

slave, would have stooped to eat or drink in a wineshop. For they used to study dignity, not vulgarity.' And Hypereides in the speech *Against Patrocles*...says that the Areopagites debarred anyone who had lunched in a wineshop from being promoted to the Court of the Areopagus. But you, my professor of wisdom, wallow in the wineshops."

(Cynulcus, in Athenaeus's *The Deipnosophists*)

Yet, even if owing to my stooping habit I never find a better Patrian dive, I do not think I will ever go far wrong for my vulgarity. That, anyway, is the sort of uncertainty that draws the non-codifying wine slave back to Patras.

PART III

IONIAN ISLANDS

IONIAN ISLANDS

(23) Zakynthos
(24) Cephalonia
(25) Ithaca
(26) Corfu

23

SOCIETY PAGES

Not even my long acquaintance with the raw populism, not to say egalitarian incivility, that the Greeks generally perpetrate on each other in public situations touching on their inalienable rights – or in which they sense a pie is being divvied up and someone else might take the slice due them – prepared me for my first quarter-hour on Zakynthos.

My daughter and I had just arrived on the island by ferry from Kilini, southwest of Patras. The same bus that brought us from Athens to Kilini also made the ferry ride and took us from the pier to the bus company's little one-story depot in the town of Zakynthos. We went into the dumpy and cramped structure, which was also part snack shop and part tourist shop, to make a phone call to a contact who could arrange accommodations for us.

The telephone was as public as could be, just a tabletop telephone set out on an open counter, but I had it all to myself when I stepped over to make my call. But after speaking to my party for perhaps three minutes, a grandmotherly matron to my rear, who had not come into my field of vision at all, began pestering me volubly to get off the phone so she could use it. Since I was in the middle of getting crucial informa-

Greek Salad

tion I ignored her, which to her obviously democratic frame of mind must have been an affront more fundamentally hurtful to her than my continued possession of the phone receiver. She began jostling me and beating me on the back with her purse, and finally went and brought a man, presumably the manager, who asked me to yield the phone. I stood my ground defiantly for another full minute until I had all the instructions I needed from my contact. At no time did the woman claim an emergency situation, and as it turned out, she had nothing more urgent to do than to call a taxi to take her home. And her home was, as we saw when we passed by in our own taxi as she was being discharged, less than a kilometer down the road.

This, I thought, should not have happened in the Ionian islands. Other Greeks think of the Ionian islanders, who spent practically no time under the degrading rule of the Ottomans, as having breeding: "the true politeness, the nobility, of the Ionian, which can have the same quality whether it pertains to a count or to a shepherd" (Ilias Venezis, *In the Greek Seas*). Least of all did I expect a breech of civility on Zakynthos, where remnants of Byzantine and Italian aristocracy had flourished for several centuries under Venetian rule.

*

I was long overdue in going to Zakynthos. I had meant to visit about five years earlier to meet my pen friend, Count Comoutos, who was producing and bottling wines at his estate. But he died and I postponed my visit several years more. Of course, though, a visit to the Comoutos estate, Agria, remained at the top of my list of things to do on Zakynthos, and the Count's widow, who knew of my correspondence with her late husband, invited us to come out for a visit one afternoon, which we did.

My eyes were peeled for Agria from the time we passed a sign for Macherado, the nearest village. I recognized the estate as soon as it was within eyeshot, from a printed sketch of it that the Count had sent me once. A neat, laterally arranged collection of low-lying buildings, Agria could pass for a California ranch complex even though it is at home on the flat plain of Zakynthos. The country residences of the Zakynthian nobility historically took their stylistic cues from Italy, but Agria was built after the 1953 earthquake that obliterated most physical reminders of old Zakynthos.

Agria was now supervised by Countess Comoutos's brother, who met us upon our arrival and immediately took us on a tour of the vineyard and cellar. We began at a small grove where some ancient members of the Comoutos family were buried beneath illegible gravestones that stood askew as a result of the earthquakes they had withstood over the centuries. The Comoutos family had been residing at Agria since

Greek Salad

1638. They were the uppermost crust of the old Za-kynthian aristocracy:

>…I have known on Zakynthos four persons who depart from the ordinary rule. The Count of Scilla, Count Combuto [sic], Doctor Ruidi, and Samuel Strani have studied in Italy, and foreigners who would go to this island should not miss becoming acquainted with them; they are a phenomenon for this country, and perhaps would be anywhere else…After them, abandon the hope of meeting others: in general, one is repulsed by the appear-ance of the Zakynthians, and one laments their stu-pidity.
>
> (Saverio Scrofani, 1801)

I was given a poster of the Comoutos coat of arms when we finished the tour and were leaving the winery building.

We went directly from the winery to meet the Countess. She led us into a dated but elegant drawing room on the second floor of the house, where we sat to chat and have a bowl of ice cream. We were overlook-ing the vineyard, and the Countess's brother must have caught me gazing wistfully out towards it, because he pointedly commented to me from out of the blue, "It must seem very agreeable to have a property like this, but managing it takes a great deal of effort." He cer-tainly had me pegged.

Ionian Islands

It was apparent from his long letters, that Count Comoutos had relished managing Agria. He loved Zakynthian wine traditions, too. His specialty was *verdea*, a dry white wine from a mixture of grape varieties. Unlike most *verdea*, which is usually drunk young, the Count's was aged for several years until it resembled a sherry. His version dated to a time, before the democratization of island society in the early 19th century, when the Zakynthian nobility was still in a position to expend considerable time and resources on wine. He had also been interested in trying to recreate a kind of Zakynthian sweet white wine called *lianorroidi*, which had not been produced for two or three generations. Everything that is known about it suggests a wine of the landed nobility, not the peasantry. However, nothing had materialized from the Count's project at the time of his death, and *lianorroidi* most likely will rest in peace in these republican times.

*

Our visit to Zakynthos coincided with that of a Zakynthian friend, Popi, who was spending her summer vacation on her native island. Popi keeps a car on Zakynthos and one evening took us, together with her daughter and brother, to the *panayiri*, or patron saint's festival, at the mountain village of Ayia Marina. I was anxious to see the Zakynthians at their leisure. In the back of my mind I had a passage from a book that Count Comoutos sent me:

Greek Salad

Every spring the Zakynthians would set out with little bundles full of meatballs and large flasks of *verdea*…to go and listen to the nightingale of Vizantida [garden]. Some went on foot and others by boat from the side by the sea. Some went for purposes of eating and drinking, and others to refresh their warm, amorous breast by sustaining with their adroit guitars and loquacious mandolins "the same note" as the mad nightingale.

(Dionysios Romas, *About Zakynthos*)

At Ayia Marina we were just below the timberline. Looking down to the east we could see the plain of Zakynthos in all its expanse, spread out resplendently in the final glow of sunlight; and above to the west a wall of evergreen trees extended against the backdrop of the darkened mountain and affirmed Homer's habitual description of "wooded Zakynthos." The *panayiri* itself was a surfeit for the senses. Vendors in the churchyard were manning shallow caldrons that looked like steel drums of the Caribbean and were frying in them the standby of Zakynthian festivals, *fritoures* – bland blocks of semolina browned in oil and rolled in granulated sugar. The din of clanging bells brought everyone into the church for a ceremony brimming with incense and psalmody, and then a procession went all around the village. After that came the feast proper.

Ionian Islands

Popi sped off to buy roast lamb for all of us, while our daughters went for soft drinks and to watch the dancing that was to begin as soon as the three lay liturgical chanters switched to *bouzouki*, drums and electric organ. I remained behind with Popi's brother, Spiros, to guard the table and chairs. Ours was a real assignment, too, because the churchyard was packed with people, and chairs were at a premium. Several celebrators tried to spirit chairs away from our table. Spiros was feeling jovial and just shook his head and chuckled at each attempt on our chairs, as though he was tickled after not seeing the antics of his compatriot Zakynthians for a long time. He had returned to Greece only recently and reluctantly, for family reasons, after having spent several decades in Montreal, where he had grown accustomed to other social behavior. I reduced Spiros to real tears of laughter by relating my story about the woman and the telephone. "You can't fix these people," he said when he recovered himself.

Meanwhile, Popi returned with the roast lamb and wanted to know what we were laughing about. I could tell she was poised for a laugh herself. But when I told her about the chairs and the telephone, her face registered, instead, a melancholic sympathy for the Zakynthians, and she apologized, "They're insecure." My own grin was quashed. I recalled reading about Venetian times on Zakynthos, when the nobility enjoyed such legally sanctioned rights as taking their agricultural losses out of the hide of their sharecroppers, and also, if they were of a mind to (nobility is not obliged), taking the sharecroppers' brides' hides to bed on the wedding night.

We turned our attention to the roast lamb, whose presentation seemed a page torn out of Homer. The meat was sold in joints by weight, and along with a few slices of bread was laid in butcher's paper, to be carried to the table and shared in common. No utensils were available, so we tore off chunks of meat with our fingers. Lamb and bread was the only choice, too. Or rather, that is what was available for the masses. For over two hours a parade of foods various and sundry was brought out on platters and plates to the sectarian and secular dignitaries seated at the decorated tables lined up perpendicular to the church door.

Carafes of wine were also provided for the notables. I had hoped some of the village's red wine would be available at the *panayiri* because Ayia Marina traditionally was one of the island's best locales for red. But the common folk had only beer and soft drinks to choose from. The patron of Zakynthos is Saint Dionysios, but the island at some time must have lost touch with the ancient Greek notion of Dionysus: "god of the peasants, a democratic god, in contrast to the gods of the noblemen" (Ioannis Melas, *History of the Island of Ikaria*).

*

Ionian Islands

Our base of operations on Zakynthos was on the southern tail of the island plain, an entirely agricultural landscape that has shaped the economic and social history of Zakynthos ever since the Venetians planted it with currant vines five hundred years ago. Even a half-baked agriculturalist like me could appreciate the plain after a walk through some of its olive groves. The soil was soft and deep and gave the feeling of sinking into a mattress of down.

I had no particular preference to stay in that corner of the island. It was simply that our Zakynthian contact, Dimitri, brought us out that way. Although making his living in the booming local industry of constructing villas, Dimitri's heart and home were far down the dirt roads of the plain. Both he and his wife had as much of a whole-Earth outlook as is ever likely to sprout on gay Zakynthos, and they took pride in being nearly self-sufficient in food and drink. Olive and fruit trees, vines, a vegetable garden, goats and sheep, hens and chickens, rabbits and doves – these comprised the larder at their doorstep. Dimitri's special contribution was small game, especially the feathered kind. His weaponry was hung on the two-story wall by the grandiose hearth. I could not help but think of the old Zakynthian nobility, a fine gastronomical species:

> The chase was not here the reward of indefatigable labour; the [Zakynthian] nobleman enjoying luxurious ease, had his arms carried by a servant; and

Greek Salad

softly reposing in an elbow-chair, under a spreading olive-tree, expected the arrival of the turtle-doves. Books of amusement, the social conversation of friends, gentle exercise, provoked an appetite which all the science of Apicius was employed to satisfy...The philosophy of Epicurus finds here many disciples, and the pursuit of the Summum Bonum is only occasionally arrested by the alarming reports of earthquake and apoplexies.

(John Sibthorp, 1795)

The room Dimitri arranged for us was in the nearby little beach resort area of Porto Koukla. My daughter and I became very fond of indulging our own modest epicurean inclination on the hotel veranda, where we ate most of our meals. But we were frequently distracted by the ups and downs, played out in public, in the curious relationship between the two brothers who owned the hotel and their Germanic hostess; she sometimes seemed to be in the one brother's camp and sometimes the other's. I frequently felt as though I were an extra on the set of an Ionian operetta, and the more so because tiffs amongst the three usually resulted in the one brother taking his guitar and heading for the seaward railing of the veranda to unleash Italianate Zakynthian melodies. Having found my own Summum Bonum in drinking a nobly plebeian *verdea* with fried mullet and *tzatziki*, I would have sung over that and let the devil take the hostess.

Ionian Islands

Popi, her daughter and Spiros joined us at the hotel on our final evening. A local christening party came in and took over the veranda but welcomed everyone to join in the spirit and the dancing. The band played as much Western dance music as Greek, and Dimitri and his wife, who were with the christening party, were among the first to take to the floor. They ate up couples-dancing and danced promiscuously with the company, as did the other locals generally. I never saw anything like it in Greece. "People here like to have a good time," said Spiros, patting his brow with a handkerchief after coming back from the dance floor. "They don't just work."

24

ROCKS AND HARD PLACES

Cephalonia has me spooked. I have bad vibes about the place. Only our proximity on Zakynthos persuaded me to revisit with my daughter.

Nothing could have been more auspicious than the outset of my previous visit. It was a crystal clear spring afternoon and the ferry from Patras skipped over a gentle sea for four idyllic hours. I will never again be lulled into a false sense of security about Cephalonia.

That night I was awakened about 3 a.m. by what I first thought, in my semi-conscious state, must be the freighter at the quay across the street, even if it was a strange time to be getting underway. But when I looked out from the balcony I saw that the vessel was still tied up fast. Not a creature was stirring aboard her, either. I went back to bed and happily began to resume my slumber – only to be jarred once again. That was when I realized that Cephalonia itself had become a sea vessel of sorts and was being tossed about on the Ionian by serious earth tremors.

"The Earth danced a lot last night," remarked one of the practiced old locals the next morning. It had been a dance I would just as soon have sat out, and I

Ionian Islands

decided I had better be on my way lest the terrestrial orchestra strike up for its rendition of the 1812 Overture, which always leaves everyone all left feet. I was on the next ferry out of there, and even now I am much more comfortable watching the island grow smaller on a ferry's stern than larger on the bow.

Call me morbid, but I am reminded of destruction almost everywhere on Cephalonia. My daughter and I were hardly off the ferry at Pesada, on the southern coast, when we passed through the unlikely Ionian village of Kourkoumelata, which was rebuilt in neo-classical-cum-Bermuda style by an expatriate Cephalonian millionaire after the devastating earthquake of 1953 leveled practically every structure on the island.

Speaking of the millionaire, I must say, in defense of my shakiness, that the natives themselves are less than sanguine about Cephalonia. They are renowned even amongst the Greeks for their propensity to emigrate. It is not generally known, for instance, that the Juan de Fuca Strait between the state of Washington and the Canadian island of Vancouver is named, not for some Spanish explorer, but for the Cephalonian sailor Ioannis Fokas. Some suppose this wanderlust goes back to the island's days as a center of piracy. I could have believed this as I watched a veritable Blackbeard of a Cephalonian repatriate, his outlandish costume askew, trying to navigate our hotel's driveway while cradling a partially consumed whiskey bottle in one arm and waving a three-inch thick of wad of

Greek Salad

U.S. dollars in the other hand. But I am more swayed by the Kavadias brothers, who represent Cephalonia in Washington, D.C., at their restaurant on Capitol Hill and make no bones about the native obsession to escape the earthquakes. The 1953 disaster alone chased away nearly half of the population.

We passed through Kourkoumelata on the way to Calligata (one soon warms to the –ata ending of most Cephalonian village names). I had arranged a morning visit at the winery of the Calligas family, the village's namesake clan. The island's typical white wine, Robola, is Cephalonia's calling card in Greece. And the local deity is very jealous of the native juice. On my earlier visit I had been blasé about Robola. The bottles of it that I had drunk had not moved me. On the ferry's approach to the port of Sami I surveyed the bright, rocky, shrub-dappled coast without experiencing that phenomenon peculiar to wine lovers, of saliva starting to flow at the mere sight of topography which is esteemed for its wine. That night's earthquake surely was a divine rebuke.

This is not to say that Cephalonia is not sufficiently dramatic even when the terrain is not shifting under one's feet. The Calligas enologist, Yannis Alayeoryiou, drove us up onto the flanks of Mt. Aenos, the island's highest point, and the vistas along the way were striking.

Ionian Islands

The firm's main Robola vineyard is located in the mountains between Argostoli and Sami, by the hamlet of Razata. Charles Napier, an early 19th century British governor of the Ionians who resided on the island, referred to Cephalonia's "wine of stone" in his book about his years there, and I am sure he could only have meant Robola. The vines at Razata, anyway, were planted among broken up stones. But they were arranged in neat rows, which would have seemed distinctly 'modern' except that Yannis cited Homer's mention of the rows that Ulysses's father, Laertes, had in his vineyard on neighboring Ithaca, which in those times was Cephalonia's master and mentor.

Yannis also took us to the winery of Calligas's major competitor, the island cooperative. The cooperative had not yet been in operation on my earlier visit, but it was situated on familiar ground, the extensive mountain plateau of Omalai next to Mt. Aenos. I had previously been taken to Omalai by a grizzled and rugged taxi-driver, another buccaneer type, whom Chance intervened to place before me upon my arrival in Sami. He was a staunch advocate of the virtues of Robola drawn straight from the barrel. Just the casual mention to him of the bottled products I had been willing to accept as credible examples of Robola brought out a bitter stream of invective, and he vehemently offered to take me right then and there to taste what he called "pure Robola." He said it would teach me just how badly the wine is botched by the bottlers. Not wanting to be told to get out and walk from that point on the road to the still distant town of Argostoli – such was his vehemence – I saw no choice but to comply with the offer. We shortly left the main road and headed for Omalai, to Valsamata, which butts flush against Frangata.

Both villages had been totally rebuilt in a disappointingly functional and nondescript style after 1953. We entered a homely *taverna* in Valsamata operated by the cabby's crony in cups, Barba Vassili (Uncle Willie). At the very moment of our arrival Barba Vassili was readying two large demijohns of his Robola for their circuitous shipment to a customer in Athens who was not happy with any wine that might be purchased in bottle around the corner. Barba Vassili of course was another implacable foe of wine in bottles, and he and the taxi-driver clucked and harrumphed about bottled Robola for several minutes, almost as if by ritual bonding, before he went and brought out a pitcher of his own Robola and a plate of Omalai *feta* cheese. The wine proved as exceptional as the cheese and certainly was worth the detour as far as I was concerned. My uneasiness in admitting its superiority stemmed entirely from the feeling I had, which was unavoidable in that company, of appearing to underwrite their notion that a wine is better for never having seen the inside of a bottle.

The cooperative's best wine was a Robola grown in vineyards under its direct supervision. I was sure this wine could have claimed its birthright as Cephalonian even in Barba Vassili's eyes (were he blind-folded). It was named 'San Gerassimo.' The winery was practically next door to the Monastery of Ayios Gerassimos, the island's patron saint. Reversing the usual pattern, Gerassimos was a 16th century mainlander who came to Cephalonia and never left.

Gerassimos lived and died in a cellar-like cave below the monastery. I peered down into his ancient subterranean dwelling, there in the bowels of Cephalonia, and had a flashback to the earthquake that rocked me. I had thrown on my pants and flip-flops in a jiffy and scurried down to the hotel lobby. Other guests had already staked out stanchions to hug in case the overhead caved in, and were regretting that they still had days left on their Cephalonian holiday packages. Perhaps Gerassimos had a better idea. It is explained that he was merely an ascetic, but I am of the opinion that he expected an apocalypse and had some reason to think his fallout shelter a safe bet. After all, the old hole survived the 1953 earthquake even while the monastery came tumbling down around it.

The Cephalonians still have Gerassimos, too. They remove the old boy from his silver sarcophagus and parade him around the monastery grounds on his name day. My daughter was relieved when Yannis said we were still several days away from that occasion. We were told that Gerassimos is something of a prune. I could not figure out, however, why the Cephalonians place such great trust by him. Gerassimos may be the designated patron, but he did virtually nothing in 1953 other than save his own jerky again.

It was a slow period at the winery, which gave Yannis the time to befriend us. We spent a couple of evenings with him in Argostoli. I had stayed in Argostoli on my earlier visit. The taxi-driver had recommended a hotel to me there after accomplishing his mission in Omalai. The town is situated beside a long sleeve of water that extends inland from a sizeable bay, and its main streets run in rows parallel to the inlet. The hotel was at the far end of the street fronting the water. I was relieved to find the lodgings rather too newfangled for a man of the taxi-driver's antiquated convictions about wine – the hotel had electricity and running water. I was given a room directly facing a scruffy little freighter (the one that later became my seismograph) and did not squabble about it because it was conceivably the best view in town. Argostoli is just Valsamata and Frangata spread over a larger canvas.

There was an era when I probably would have delighted in Argostoli. I have read a native's account of the once thriving tradition of *taverna*s where the barrels of various local wines were tasted and compared in an atmosphere of rustic good humor. But that tradition began to go into decline during the Italian occupation in the Second World War, and the 1953 earthquake finished it off. When, on my first visit, I set out from the hotel early in the evening to survey the town's eateries, I found far slimmer pickings than I did a decade later, and no local dishes were on any menu. I ended up at a place where my choice was from several midday menu entries that had been descending to room temperature all afternoon. The owner did pour his own Robola, but it was thin and overly gassy stuff from the lowlands in back of Argostoli, not Omalai.

Afterwards I roamed the length and breadth of Argostoli but found nothing more inspiring than some palm trees and a statue of Charles Napier, the old British governor. I gave up on the town early and took a seat in the main square, where, having no thirst left for Robola, whether from bottle or barrel or even an amphora, I quaffed beer brewed under foreign license. Perhaps I am taking that night's earthquake too personally, but I believe this may have been the final straw that brought on the wrath of the genius loci.

Yannis took my daughter and me all the way to the island's northern tip. We even passed Kothreas, the hometown of the Kavadias brothers of Capitol Hill. Ruins from 1953 were still to be seen along the road. We ended up at Fiskardo, a quaint fishing port where mostly pleasure craft were tied up. The village has become the favored area for the villas of émigré Cephalonians. This is no doubt because Fiskardo was the only settlement spared by the 1953 earthquake.

We were delighted at lunch in Fiskardo to try a Cephalonian specialty, the eponymously named *kefa-*

Greek Salad

lonitikipita, a savory pie consisting of pieces of lamb with rice and herbs in an unusual crust that was not made from phyllo dough. I have subsequently suggested to the Kavadias brothers that they offer the pie on their Capitol Hill menu, but they insist that the dough for the crust cannot be duplicated without Cephalonian water. However that might be, I am nonetheless cheered that Cephalonian dishes are beginning to get as much exposure as the islanders themselves, whether Juan de Fuca, the Kavadias brothers, or even Saint Gerassimos.

25

HOMECOMING

Listless dawn dropped an olive scrim of summer haze as Ulysses of the wine jars rolled out of bed forlorn as usual in his flat above the lager-brown Potomac. For ten years he had been away from the winedark sea and in misery, caught and suffering in the gnashing wheels of Lower Bureaucracy. Not an evening passed without sacrificing a hog or sheep, or occasionally a steak, and pouring bacchic libations to the gods, but to no avail. For he was in perpetual disfavor with Dionysus and could not return to Hellas.

Athena of the fluttering eyelids saw the frustrated wine wanderer in his sedentary agony, took pity on him and went to plead his case before Zeus who carries the glorious corkscrew. "Oh, Smog-gatherer," said Athena, "Ulysses of the wine jars has endured enough. Let me spur him to return to Hellas, his vinous homeland. Or has he in some way affronted beyond all measure these Olympian halls?"

To this the Father of the Ozone Layer responded: "Decency and sensibility are what Olympians respect in men. Ten years ago yon Ulysses jangled the nerves of Dionysus by confounding the god with endless questions about what mortals call 'wine quality.' I do not know whether Dionysus in the meantime has exacted his tribute in watching the winy wretch twist and turn among his cartons of glass wine jars in that sordid flat above the lager-brown waters."

No sooner did Dionysus hear the name of his quibbling nemesis than he started from his couch and upset his cup and was at Zeus's side to add his two drachmas even before the spilled nectar had soaked through the burgundy upholstery. "I do not understand Athena's affection for dim-witted Ulysses of the wine jars, who is always ready to challenge the quality of the wine he takes from me. Is it that this eternal strumpet wants to go making her bed with a wine-besotted mortal?"

At these words the goddess let fly with stinging words for her fellow Olympian. "Mend your own leching ways, you, whose mother was a flaming mortal tramp off the streets."

Thus reminded of his origins and put in his place did Dionysus relent and growl, "Let her do as she wishes with that sorry excuse for a wine lover. But this one satisfaction I demand, that Ulysses of the wine jars make straight for Ithaca's rocky shores. Let him thirst there for a cup of native wine until he well realizes how good are all my gifts."

Athena of the fluttering eyelids stopped not even to primp but only sped over the horizon to the eerie where Ulysses sat befuddled. The goddess wasted no time, either, in taking the form of Ulysses's blossoming daughter, Telemachoula of the persistent will, and commenced nagging: "Father, for ten years you have sat there bemoaning your absence from Hellas and promising to take me one day. I am almost grown now and will not be a burden to you on the journey. I mean, like, will you stop your dithering, and let us be gone?"

Ulysses mulled over Telemachoula's words a spell with his slow wit. He was of two minds as to whether or not to dither further. Athena then caused a big ugly blackbird to fly down and tear at the flesh of a possum carcass in the driveway below the flat. Thus reminded of his own mortality, Ulysses of the wine jars said to the cheeky Telemachoula: "Certainly you must be speaking with the authority of the immortal ones, and so I have no choice but to take you to Hellas. But where in that land of a trillion amphora shards shall we go? What wine do I need to taste there?"

Athena had her answer at the ready and was out with it at once through the mouth of Telemachoula of the fashion accessories: "To Ithaca, Father. Look, I am already reading *The Odyssey* for school next year. Would that I could shop for beads and sandals where Penelope did."

The ten-year prisoner of Lower Bureaucracy was stirred when he heard the name of the fabled island, and he rushed off at once to a travel agency.

Greek Salad

Meanwhile, Dionysus had caused evil times to befall Ithaca. The wine-god was fuming at the Ithacans for neglecting the fine rows of vines they once kept. Long gone were the days that he so fondly remembered, when the cellar of an Ithacan king could be tapped day after day for years on end to dissolve cholesterol for a perpetually feasting army of suitors. It was the rare Ithacan who bothered with vines at all any longer. The Ithacans now preferred to live by turning somersaults for the red-breasted sojourners from the northern lands and cashing remittances from overseas kinfolk. And as for their drink, they had taken to the foaming brews. For no less provocation did Dionysus smote the Ithacans with a disastrous vintage the previous growing season.

All unawares of the wine-god's meddling, and of what was in store for himself, Ulysses of the wine jars, with Telemachoula in tow, steamed out over the salt sea on an Aetolian ferry from Astakos to rugged Ithaca one July morning as the sun climbed toward its garish midsummer display. A channel led into the island's hidden bay of Phorcys and passed by the hillocks in front of the two beaches where the red-breasted sojourners from the northern lands were spread-eagling themselves to acquire their full tint.

The Aetolian vessel docked and the winy traveler stepped ashore and ventured his thoughts: "I may be dim-witted, but not half as much as the German classicist who launched the hapless theory that Homer's

Ionian Islands

Ithaca was not the modern one. (Or else, was he an utter landlubber?) How could he fail to recognize this dramatic roadstead as the place from which the ancients set sail for the dark mainland with the west wind behind them, as Homer told?" But no one was listening, for the practical Telemachoula was already halfway down the vehicular roadway towards town and accommodations.

Now, in the chief town of Vathy, at the head of the bay, Ithacan caterers were carving joints and tending gridirons day and night to keep the encamped fair-haired horde larded and returning. Among them was Eumaeus of the scraggly beard, whose awning was spread in a narrow lane off the waterfront. Eumaeus himself caught Ulysses by the camera strap and recommended the viands of his establishment: "It is a true kitchen of rugged Ithaca that operates on this spot. You will not taste the likes of our viands anywhere else on the whole island. We are unsullied by either the cow's butter that the red-breasted sojourners from the northern lands spread or the ketchup poured by our own emigrant Ithacans returning from Queens."

Ulysses quaked with gustatory joy at these words and gratefully took a seat under Eumaeus's awning. "But tell me," asked the vinous wanderer, "you do have *tserepa*, the native dish, and some of the true un-blended juice of Ithaca with which to wash it down, do you not? For what other offering will the Olympians accept now that they have plunked me down here on rugged Ithaca?"

"Ah, *tserepa*," replied Eumaeus in doleful tones. "Last month we slaughtered our last lamb of the season for the fair-haired horde, and now *tserepa* has been struck from our menu. This kitchen is strictly kosher in its Ithacan offerings, and no meat other than lamb or kid will touch our *tserepa* pot. Let me suggest instead a fish cold there on the ice, which was swimming out beyond the channel until today's dawn. And for wine I must give you the pale kind from Lefkas, which lies towards the north and the gloom, since Dionysus has smote our vineyards and left us nary a drop of our own honey-colored vintage."

Ulysses, Puller of Corks, was as profoundly troubled by Eumaeus's last words as he had been overjoyed by his first ones. For he now remembered the wine-god and having run afoul of him ten years earlier. Ulysses swallowed hard and settled for the Lefkadite vintage. Then he steeled himself and went to take a gander at the fish. He noted them to be unclouded of eye, ruddy at the gills and firm of flesh, and so he had Eumaeus take one to the pan to broil.

The fish arrived at the table in a wash of its own juices mingled with olive oil and scant fresh herbs, and was shortly reduced to a mound of bones and scales by Ulysses, who commented for the edification of Telemachoula: "Not since I was last in this country did I eat fish which was the very essence of the stuff it is. I had forgotten that none of the foods the Hellenes cook is so often brought to the perfect expression of itself as is fish in the hands of a simple master like this scraggly bearded Eumaeus, who understands the creatures of the deep as he does his own self and reveres their qualities no less. I should think Poseidon himself could not have placed a better order, and I do hope the god persuades his immortal colleagues to accept this low-fat offering."

The long-inured Telemachoula just shrugged and went on with her Lotus-Eater Special of vegetarian stuffed tomatoes and Panhellenic salad.

The pale Lefkadite wine did its work and gave flow to Ulysses's slow wits. He took it into his head to surprise the notables at the town hall in Vathy and fling at them a quiver of questions about Ithacan wine and where to find some. But the town clerk, formerly of Teaneck, New Jersey, had discouraging words: "Nobody ever comes to Ithaca and asks about wine. We cannot answer your questions – and we cannot pour you any Ithacan wine, either. Our vines, which formerly were great in extent and reputation, are few and unsung now, and last year Dionysus, for reasons only the immortal ones comprehend, smote our remaining vineyard parcels. But here, have this list of our bed-and-breakfasts."

Greek Salad

The enological wanderer turned and left the town hall in disgust, and said to his increasingly impatient offspring: "After ten years of tribulation in Lower Bureaucracy I should have known better than to expect anything from these pathetic functionaries. We will quit Vathy and go north to Pilikata, to the Hill of Hermes, where the three mountains meet and the three seas are espied, as Homer says. For that is where the ancient city was, and I am sure that born-and-bred Ithacans still tend vines there in number."

"Yeah, right," retorted the smart aleck Telemachoula.

Ulysses of the wine jars thereupon hired four wheels for the journey and stowed jars of Perrier. The two travelers sped north over the isthmus that joins rugged Ithaca's two heaps of rocks and passed in the lee of Mount Neriton until they approached Pilikata and reached the intersection where the three menus of cyclopean proportions hang aloft. The air was tinged with the divine smell of charcoal and burning fat, and Ulysses's heart leapt when he made out the words LOCAL WINE on one of the menus. "Here I can make a proper offering to the Olympians," he declared simplemindedly.

The vinous wanderer ordered a score of dainties fit for a royal prince and a measure of the true unblended juice of Ithaca. Presiding over the premises was stubby Arnaeus, who overheard Ulysses and stepped over and said in English of the Australian sort, "Alas, we have no Ithacan wine this year. Dionysus smote our berries and I don't think you will find any native wine anywhere on the island. How about a beer, mate?"

"That will never do," answered Ulysses of the wine jars. "It dawns on me that we are all in hot water with the wine-god as it is. Just hold the dainties and instead bring me a roasted goat's paunch stuffed with fat and blood. If it was good enough for unrequited suitors, it will be good enough for me."

Ulysses, Puller of Corks, became morose digesting the paunch and thinking that for the first time in his Hellenic wine travels he would find no native wine at all, whether good, bad or indifferent. He began sobbing inconsolably. He did not stop until Telemachoula of the fashion accessories left to look at the trinkets being sold across the way and Athena of the fluttering eyelids came and took his daughter's seat and braced him up.

"Are you dim-witted or something?" said the Daughter of Zeus who carries the glorious corkscrew. "Get a hold of yourself. Any fool can see that Dionysus has his fingers in this dish of circumstances, and you shall have to outsmart him."

"I'll be damned!" exclaimed Ulysses. "It is clear from your true blond roots that you are Athena herself, and not one of these ordinary mortal Greek skirts. Or else the paunch has caused more havoc in my head than it has in my stomach."

"I am indeed the goddess," continued Athena, "and that paunch has nothing to do with it. (But I must tell you, not even in the old days could I fathom what mortals saw in that dish, though I suppose it was fare fit for a loitering bunch of no-account suitors.) Anyway, listen to me carefully. What you must do is go back south to Vathy, ascend Mount Neion to the village of Perahorion and visit Eurycleia's grill, where there remains a jar of wine from the well-tended vineyard of Laertes, who is awaiting the return of his son, the one who owns the dozen diners on Long Island. Then you shall have the true unblended juice of Ithaca. But first take care to disguise yourself and your blossoming daughter as red-breasted sojourners from the northern lands, so that the wine-god, when he sees you, will not distinguish you from the rest of the fair-haired horde and do anything that might thwart your quest."

The next day, as dawn drew back its florid tentacles from over the salt sea, Ulysses and Telemachoula fortified themselves with currant buns and yogurt. Once the fiery orb of the heavens was well into its ascent, the pale visitors stretched out in its sapping radiance until they glowed with rosiness. Not until the blistering brightness began to abate later in the day did the travelers trek up Mount Neion. They climbed for half an hour in the wrong footwear, with only the scent of wild thyme as a balm for their spirit.

"Don't you ever get tired of tasting wine?" jabbed the wilting Telemachoula on a rest stop.

Eurycleia was firing up the grill for the evening trade when the twosome entered her place in Pera-horion. The winy traveler approached her and inquired whether she had any native wine, to which she responded: "You must be the wine-thirsty stranger the blond strumpet with the fluttering eyelids told me about in my dream last night. Well, you're in luck, because the grower Laertes managed to harvest a few grapes and make a bit of wine last year, and we've still got an amphora of it here. Just take a seat on a bench outside and I'll bring you a cup of it." Then she noticed Ulysses's feet and added: "But if you ask me, you probably need salve for your feet more than you need wine." As she left to get the wine, Eurycleia mumbled, "Only a dimwit would wear anything but sandals on rugged Ithaca."

Ulysses, Puller of Corks, drank deeply and thankfully from the honey-colored wine of Ithaca and gazed at the splendorous view towards the north and the gloom. Grilled fowl was offered up in abundance at Eurycleia's that evening, and the pantheon reveled in the high-drifting smoke.

26

CLASSICS

All of us are prone to do a lot of supposing when it comes to ancient Greece. "I suppose," wrote Mark Twain, for one, "that ancient Greece and modern Greece compared furnish the most extravagant contrast to be found in history" (*The Innocents Abroad*). The Dionysian traveler, however, can expect gooseflesh to rise every so often because of something seen or heard or otherwise experienced in the Greece of the present day.

In a small *taverna* on Corfu, for instance, a man of venerable age plunged me back a good 1,800 years or so. He entered the *taverna*, approached the counter and ordered a tumbler of white wine. Then he embarked on a preliminary examination of it that was as masterful as any that side of the Chevaliers du Tastevin. After looking at the filled glass intently in the little bit of light he had, he sniffed around its nearly topped-off rim for what seemed an eternity – really so long that anyone looking could have thought the old gent's joints had locked. But suddenly there was a resurgence of movement. The creaking arm brought the glass to the lips of the now cocked-back head, and the wine went down in one long, gulping draught. The man then lowered the glass and for several extended moments, as if a-wallow in the wine's aromatic savor, smacked his lips while staring straight ahead at the wall behind the counter. Having taken his pleasure in full, he set the tumbler down, turned around and left. Could a classicist fail to recall 'the breathless cup' remarked on by Athenaeus, who described it as "a sort of drinking which is to be accomplished without taking a breath or closing the mouth"?

The virtuoso performance was given in the lower-class Garitsa quarter on the southern fringe of Corfu Town, at a distance from the Italianate nucleus. The *taverna* was called Lefkimmi and was a hangout for taxi-drivers, to which I was brought by my guide, Nikos, a taxi-driver. We sampled both the red and the white wine that were on tap and agreed on the white as the one to have with lunch, although we as yet had no idea as to what we would eat. By consenting to Nikos's inversion of the cosmopolitan rule of selecting the wine *after* deciding upon the food, I may have sunk even below those regulars at the Lefkimmi who altogether dodge modern questions of wine and food etiquette by taking their meals at home and coming in for a tumbler of wine only afterward. The Corfiotes, after all, might at least be acting on advice that has in some form come down from antiquity. "The ancients," noted Plutarch about a generation much earlier than even his own, "did not even drink water before the dessert course, but nowadays people get themselves intoxicated before eating a thing" (*Table-talk*).

Greek Salad

Worse yet, after consulting the proprietor-cook but not me, Nikos unilaterally ordered *bourtheto* for both of us. The problem was that *bourtheto*, a Corfiote fish dish prepared in a skillet with a thin tomato sauce, has a bit of 'hot' paprika added to it. I could imagine epicures from my clime pointing the finger at me for drinking an unexceptionable wine, which the white was, with a slightly caustic dish. But Nikos reckoned this combination the very thing. He touched his fingers to his lips as he relished a sip of the wine after a bite of the fish and said, "How nicely it burns." But that was not the half of it. He also claimed that the flavor of the wine was *enhanced* by the *bourtheto*. This was nothing short of heresy to wine folks back where I live. Yet Nikos was reminiscent of Plutarch's table companion Symmachus recommending the burn of another condiment, salt: "moderately salty foods, on account of their pleasant taste, bring out the sweetness and smoothness of any kind of wine." Salt, like pepper, was understood by the ancient Greeks to belong to the realm of 'hot' (*thermoi*) and 'heating' (*thermantikoi*) substances.

The wines at the Lefkimmi were from the *taverna*'s namesake village in the deep south of the island. North and south count for a lot on Corfu because the island is composed of a northern highland and southern lowland to which the natives attribute sharply divergent effects on human character. Lawrence Durrell, in *Prospero's Cell*, noted that in the 1930s Corfiotes still harbored strong prejudices against compatriots from the opposite parts of the island, including opposition to intermarriage. The quality of agricultural products is still viewed through this lens. For instance, according to northerners, all of the island's best wines come from their upland vineyards. Nikos hotly disputed this contention and took me to the Lefkimmi expressly to prove his point. He was confident because the wines offered at the *taverna* were his father's.

I had not expected much of Corfu where wine is concerned, whether in the north or in the south. Except for a Corfiote lawyer who had written a book about the island in the 1950s and judiciously praised all the wines, I had not found any very complimentary reference to Corfiote wine later than Xenophon's mention that Mnassipos's Lacedaemonian troops found excellent wine on the island. But what would Spartans have known about taste, anyhow? Athenians of my acquaintance were uncharacteristically unanimous in branding Corfiote wine: they grimaced, stuck out their tongue or made rude noises at its mere mention – and this was from swillers of *retsina*. It did not take long on Corfu to discover what was behind the chagrin.

I was staying at Paleokastritsa on the southwestern coast of the northern highland. Durrell had influenced me to go there by describing a jewel of a cove where he used to swim. I eventually did find a swimming hole I liked beyond all others I have enjoyed – whether or not it was Durrell's – but to my dismay the area

Greek Salad

generally was so overgrown with deluxe hotels that I could scarcely find anything to evoke the overall impression of Paleokastritsa that Durrell left with me. But on one walk in search of his cove I came upon several old pastel buildings and a few beachside vineyards that charmingly offered a composite *paysage* of Bermuda and the Mediterranean. I was drawn further into the distance by a spit of land that ended in a sizeable green protuberance, a gigantic rock covered with trees. Out there I found an older vision of Corfu in the shape of an ancient shepherdess who was wearing the native headdress, a droopy, several-cornered cabbage cover, and leading with her crook a bleating flock of *feta* on the hoof.

But if it was paleo-Corfu that was poured into my tumbler for dinner back at my hotel later on, I would just as soon have left it for more appreciative visitors from Lacedaemon. It was a sweet-sour red wine that stood at a remove from my notion of 'good.'

Nikos subsequently took me through villages on the highland above Paleokastritsa where nothing but sweet-sour wines were being offered by peasants at their makeshift roadside stands. These petty entrepreneurs also proferred samplings of almonds. This seemed to be their sales tactic that comes closest to the ploy of 'selling over cheese' that the wine merchants of northern lands once practiced to impart a more flattering savor to their wines by way of the lingering aftertaste of the cheese. But the Corfiote habit might not be entirely mercenary and could be as old as 'the breathless cup.' According to Plutarch, "the bitterness of almonds is naturally helpful against wine, for it dries up the inside of the body and does not let the veins become full." Over almonds, anyway, not all of the wine samples tasted poorly, and in the spirit of further inquiry I took away a few bottles of them, some red, some white and some indefinite in color.

At one village I left my Greek islander's straw hat on the roof of the taxi and had forgotten about it when we were finished tasting and I climbed back in. As we started to drive away the hat did a flip in the air, flew back in through the window on the passenger side and landed squarely in my lap, crown side up. Nikos, who had tasted everything except the almonds and bought nothing, marveled at this and with ancient faith read the sight as an omen that would require some sort of practical interpretation. At our next stop, the village of Makrades, he went straight for the open-air sales table attendant who was wearing the same kind of straw hat as my charmed one. While they conversed I tried the wares of the other hopefuls. All the wines again were sweet-sour, in whatever color might suit the purchaser.

I had to wonder about these wines. Could they be a holdover from antiquity? Athenaeus referred to an early time when salt was not used in Greece, and this period must have given rise to characteristic types of wine. The sweet-sour wines, for instance, would not have needed the piquancy of salted food to "bring out," as Symmachos put it, their "sweetness and smoothness." But these ruminations led to the more vexing question of whether, in the greater scheme of things, the Corfiotes are one up on us in wine quality since our preferred wines have been created for palates skewed by salt. I had no satisfying answer to either question.

Nikos introduced me to the remaining seller, Mr. Pipuris, a diminutive oldster whose name delighted Nikos because it suggested something like 'pip-squeak.' Pipuris said I should go ahead and taste the wines that he had sitting out, while he went over to his ramshackle shed nearby to bring another wine. The wines on the stand proved no different than those of-fered by the competition. From the shed, however, Pipuris retrieved a demijohn of wine that Nikos per-suaded him to let us sample. It was a completely dry white wine, and of some stature, its producer notwith-standing. Pipuris was willing to sell us only a bottle each of it since this wine, rather than the sweet-sour wines, was what *he* usually drank. As far as he could tell, he said, the sweet-sour wines are what the tourists want. This certainly demonstrated what Mark Twain might have called one of "the most extravagant" in-stances of a lack of communications between produc-ers and consumers in the history of merchandising.

Makrades put me in the mood for a walk in the countryside. I had Nikos drop me off in the village of Lakones, also on the highland, while he took my wine

purchases back to the hotel. I chose Lakones in particular because I wanted to taste the village's "volcano's blood" that Durrell intriguingly described as "a
wine that bubbles ever so slightly; an undertone of
sulphur and rock." But the spell of my hat evidently
had worn off by then, because I did not find quite what
I was hoping for; or else I am not as adept as Durrell
was in detecting sulfur and carbonic gas. However, I
did taste a very dry red wine that pleased me well
enough that I bought a liter's worth of it.

The narrow road from Lakones back to Paleokastritsa wound its way down through what appeared
from some angles as a primeval forest of olive trees.
Only the stone retaining walls clearly marked out the
groves of six- and seven-hundred-year-old trees as a
feat of civilization. The density of the trees muffled
both light and sound and created a special calm. It was
utterly silly of me not to sit down against one of the
marvelously gnarled trunks and take a few draughts of
Lakones to ponder better the ancient bond between
olives, brine and wine in the Mediterranean world.

I was not sorry to be on the walk alone. But neither did I regret a meeting I had just in the middle of
my descent. It was a quaint meeting, appropriate to
the place. I was hailed from a little distance by an elderly Englishman accompanied by his wife. We continued speaking at some remove, too. Perhaps a quarter-of-an-hour passed that way. The couple had not
known they were headed for Lakones, and they would

not have learned it then, either, had the man not wondered aloud as to why a foreigner on holiday would be in the middle of these ancient groves carrying a queer beverage bottle full to its screw-cap with wine. As I had no explanation worth hearing, I deflected the question by saying something about the wine's birthplace up the road.

The fellow next wanted to know whether the wine was good. Unable any longer simply to call a wine good and feel satisfied, I started saying more about it than was needed in that setting. Fortunately I came to my senses in midstream, caught myself up short and rescued my self-respect.

The couple had not noticed. The only response I provoked was a salutary one. The man embarked on a soliloquy on our reaction to things, such as a wine, about which we ask questions like whether or not they are 'good'? We can, he said, find what is 'wrong' in anything if we choose to assess; and if we do so choose, we then must also choose either to stare at what is wrong and lament it, or look at what is 'right' and appreciate that. I had to wonder whether the archaic scenery where we were standing had inspired him, because his words resounded quietly with truth as an ancient Greek philosopher would have recognized it: "the truth," said Epictetus, "is something immortal and eternal, and does not present us with a beauty that withers from the passage of time."

Ionian Islands

As for the Englishman's own practice, it was unmistakable when he said they would continue on up to Lakones and drink some of its wine: "I shan't think it's bad, you know."